Flexibility in Constitutions

Europa Law Publishing, Groningen 2002

Flexibility in Constitutions

Forms of closer cooperation in federal and non-federal settings; post Nice edition

Annette Schrauwen (Editor)

The Hogendorp Papers (2)

Proceedings of the Annual Colloquium of the
G.K. van Hogendorp Centre for European Constitutional Studies

Europa Law Publishing is a publishing company
specializing in European Union Law.
For further information please contact Europa Law Publishing via email: info@europalawpublishing.com or visit our website at: www.europalawpublishing.com.

Typeset in Scala and Scala Sans, Graphic design by G2K Designers, Groningen/Amsterdam

NUGI 698; ISBN 90-76871-06-x

British Library Cataloguing-in-Publication Data
A catalogue record for this book is available from the British Library

Contents

CHAPTER I

Problematic Possibilities

dr. Annette Schrauwen

1 Introduction

The Treaty of Amsterdam's closer cooperation paragraphs had the merit of putting a long standing practice of diversity not only into a new straightjacket but also into a new perspective. However it also created new sources of confusion. The Treaty of Nice brought some modifications but no great clarification, leaving the latter to legal practice and, in its absence, to scholarship.

This is the challenge picked up by the present book. Its specific approach is to find analogies for these novel EU techniques of flexibility in past of existing but experienced constitutional systems, either confederate or federal. It is originally drawn from papers and discussion in the 1998 Hogendorp Colloquium, further developed from the questions raised at that occasion and from the adaptations of the Treaty of Nice.

The book combines legal analysis with historical detail.

In this book, you will find a presentation of the numerous contexts of flexible cooperation. Part I goes from the Dutch Republic of the United Provinces (*Roel Pieterman*, Law, Erasmus University Rotterdam), to the actual situation in Belgium, Spain, the French Republic and the Commonwealth of Independent States (*Bruno De Witte*, European Law, Rijksuniversiteit Limburg). In between, other contributions discuss flexibility in the German constitution (*Gerard van Wissen*, Law, University of Amsterdam), in the Swiss constitution (*Flora Goudappel*, Dutch Ministry of Justice) and in the United States (*Tim Conlan*, George Mason University, Fairfax, USA).

In Part II, short comments are made on the institutionalisation of flexibility (*Annemarie Lansdaal*, Humanities, University of Amsterdam) and on the closer cooperation paragraphs of the Amsterdam and Nice Treaties (*Annette Schrauwen*, Law, University of Amsterdam). These lead to discussions on the particularities of European Union flexibility. In her second contribution, *Flora Goudappel* deals with the institutional balance of EC and EU. *Elies Steyger* (European Administrative law, Vrije Universiteit, Amsterdam) tackles the *acquis communautaire* and *Margreth de Bonth* (Law, Tilburg University) ends Part II by presenting flexibility as an expression of sovereignty.

The main topics to come out of the debates were

1) the necessity of leadership or dominance in closer cooperation projects;
2) the usefulness of the flexibility provisions;
3) the control and transparency of enhanced cooperation forms;
4) the way they lead to unity or diversity.

These issues come together in the epilogue by *W.T. Eijsbouts*, (European Law, University of Amsterdam) who, notwithstanding all complexity, detects a model of 'balanced constitution'.

2 Dominance

The theme of dominance forms the basis of the Dutch Republic of the United Provinces (1579-1795), but in a rather paradoxical way: though Holland was the dominant force, many times in fact and in practice it was not dominant. This brings *Roel Pieterman* to express some doubts about the necessity of a dominant force for cooperation. Holland certainly held a dominant position in the Dutch Republic, but efforts were being made within the Estates General to create a countervailing power against Holland all the time. European Union history shows a comparable effort by the French in their pushing for the euro in order to countervail the dominance of the German mark.

De Witte points to the dangers inherent in too flexible a system, as is presented by the CIS: it is a tool of Russia to exercise its dominance over the other partners. Within the European Union context, the theme of dominance is taken up by the 'hard core' proposal of Lamers and Schäuble and this might have been the reason that all member states took interest in the concept of flexibility, as *Annemarie Lansdaal* argues. In a very same way, Chirac's proposal of a 'pioneer-group' served by a 'secretariat', presented in his address to the Bundestag on 27 June 2000, has ensured that flexibility got a high profile in the discussions leading up to Nice.

The example of the United States, described by *Tim Conlan*, may lead one to think that in a federation it will always be the powerful parts that use flexibility to force their will upon the others. During the discussions however, it became clear that there are examples of small states that went ahead by creating political innovations and were followed by the large states later on. One example would be welfare reform in the United States. A few states, like Wisconsin, largely developed and experimented with welfare reform. Because the experiment was considered effective, it was adopted into national law.

A dominant force is not a precondition for flexible cooperation. The dominant force of Holland sometimes even hindered the Republic in its functioning. Discussions in the Second Chamber on the judiciary showed such envy against Holland, that the only way to go was to to create a Court of Law in every Province. Nevertheless, Holland could not always exercise its dominant position, because Holland itself was a coalition of smaller forces, namely cities. As soon as discord arose among the cities, there could hardly be a strong position for Holland. The parallel in European Union context would be Germany, where the *Länder* may constrain and determine what the federal level can decide on European level.

Flexibility can also be seen as a way to refrain dominant forces from forming a 'hard core'. The inclusion of closer cooperation provisions in the treaty links the dominant states to the institutional framework of the EU. It assures that all members can eventually participate.

3 Necessity and usefulness

Roel Pieterman emphasises the pragmatic aspect of flexible cooperation: it was needed to ensure sovereignty for each province. *Tim Conlan* also points to the pragmatic aspect in his examples of cooperation between some American States, *e.g.* on transportation and watering. He feels flexibility is clearly one way of dealing with the problems of diversity that has been relatively successful in the US context. *Bruno De Witte* subscribes to the pragmatic character of flexibility; he is convinced that flexible cooperation is always introduced because of political necessity, never for its own sake. Thus, flexibility was introduced in the EU system because in its absence protagonists would be blocked and have recourse to forms outside the Treaties.

The strict conditions Amsterdam attached to flexibility provisions seem to have been inserted in order to ensure the provisions were not used in a lightly manner. In practice, they haven't been used at all in the period between Amsterdam and Nice. If the initial purpose of the negotiators was to see how exactly flexibility worked and how it could be improved in Nice, they failed. The trigger mechanism for flexibility in the first pillar is so hard; it is an emergency brake that can be applied by any single member state. Tony Blair brought it into the Treaty in the final stage of the Amsterdam negotiations. Most authors are convinced that it blocks the use of the flexibility provisions in the first pillar. It was one of the main reasons why the Nice Treaty relaxed the trigger mechanism.

Although the strict conditions on flexibility provided in the first pillar may ensure that these provisions are not used very often, the stronger and stricter framework for cooperation required by the flexibility clauses is appreciated as an attempt to constitutionalise efforts of cooperation. *De Witte* warns against a too flexible constellation. He bases his warning on an analysis of the CIS, which is a very flexible system but which cannot offer 'the same benefits of one ordered public policy that you can find in a more integrated system like the EU'. The example of Spain on the other hand is the most positive example of a clever use of flexibility so far. Part of the success of integrating Spain and having it integrated into the European Union is the choice for flexibility.

4 Transparency and control

It seems fair to state that nearly all contributors see lack of transparency and accountability as possible problems of flexible cooperation. *Gerard van Wissen* signals problems in controlling flexible cooperation (who took the decision) and draws for examples on the German experience. *Bruno De Witte* remarks that complexity comes in two forms: symmetrical and asymmetrical; it is the asymmetrical form that is represented by flexibility. He shows that federal as well as unitary systems contain elements of flexibility, though not always to the same extent.

Asymmetrical forms of flexibility surely are less transparent, or 'readable' as *Elies Steyger* calls it. She states that increasing complexity of EU law endangers its application and control. The unclear connection between all the different kinds of flexibility agreements makes one wonder whether anyone can keep up with it. *De Witte* takes the opposing view. He thinks of the EU's flexibility provisions as an effort to discipline relations between member states and the Union, that enhance the control and the transparency of forms of cooperation which otherwise would take place *outside* the scope of the European Union. The inclusion of flexibility seems to cause different problems according to the system in which it is included. In a system that is an international organisation on an intergovernmental basis like the Commonwealth of Independent States, flexibility can lead to political problems rather than legal problems. In a system like the European Union, flexibility might be politically necessary, but causes problems of control.

Accountability for closer cooperation forms should emerge from the institutional balance. It is therefore very interesting to know what the impact of the flexibility clauses on the institutional balance will be. *Flora Goudappel* rightly points out that the effect depends on the pillar under which decisions are taken. Generally, she is not very optimistic as to the accuracy with which the Amsterdam negotiators dealt with the institutional balance in the flexibility procedures. She feels that changes in the balance might be unforeseen, and even going against the reinforcement of the position of the European Parliament.

Nice brought some improvement for the European Parliament. Still, its weaker position in closer cooperation procedures might induce it to challenge the legality of any act based upon the flexibility provisions in order to obtain annulment.

5 Unity or diversity

Whereas the transparency perspective leads to critical remarks on flexibility, contributors are not so negative on the consequences of flexible cooperation for the integration process. The champion of optimism is *Margreth de Bonth,* who states at the end of her contribution that flexibility 'is one of the catalytic forces moving the integration process.' Not every author shares her vision, though the Swiss example leads *Goudappel* to say that 'closer cooperation is a necessary means for a new pre-federal structure to grow towards a closer integration'.

This vision is put in perspective by the general statement of *Van Wissen* that there usually is a strong tendency in newly formed federations to centralise powers and competencies. On the other hand, he signals that in response, members of the federation strongly defend their remaining competencies. Within Germany, the competencies of the *Länder* have been shrinking since 1949, while from Brussels the impression is that the *Länder* are becoming stronger. *Van Wissen* signals that the fact that there are so many *Länder* leads to centralisation. It is not certain, however, that the same tendency will occur in an enlarged EU; centralisation in a very large constellation is more difficult, as the example of the Roman Empire shows. Besides, the EU has a linguistic diversity that Germany does not have.

Against this background, the question whether the European Union still is a pre-federal structure becomes all the more interesting. The tendency to centralisation seems to have stopped, thereby putting an end to the federal future of Europe. The British refusal to put the 'terrible f-word' into the Treaty is in retrospect an indication of new paths the Union is taking. The substitute given in Article 1 EU Treaty, 'an ever closer union among the peoples of Europe' does certainly not stand for federation. However *Goudappel* shows that the die is not yet cast. She shows on the one hand that the first pillar flexibility provisions give Council and Parliament a more marked position as federal institutions, and on the other hand, that the third pillar flexibility provisions will stimulate intergovernmental actions instead of supranational ones.

The question whether flexibility leads to unity or diversity in the EU emerges also at the substantive level. One of the conditions is for closer cooperation not to affect the *acquis communautaire*. In first pillar matters, it might be easy to determine whether a specific measure is compatible or not with existing community law. But, as *Elies Steyger* demonstrates, it is hard to think of a flexible cooperation scheme that will not in some way hinder the internal market. In such a case, anybody who has standing before the Court of Justice may raise the point. The Nice amendment that closer cooperation provisions are not part of the *acquis communautaire* is an attempt at clarification which brings no solution.

6 Conclusion

Having read all contributions to this volume, one could reach the conclusion that flexibility is not a leap into the dark, but a necessary evil. It is a prerequisite for progress in European integration, even though no one knows what the eventual outcome will be. In their report to the Commission on the Institutional Implications of Enlargement, the three wise men - Jean-Luc Dehaene, Richard von Weizsäcker and Lord Simon of Highbury -, conclude that in 'a larger and more diverse Union, flexibility in the institutional framework is even more important than at present'.

CHAPTER II

Unity and Diversity: Flexibility in a Historical Perspective

The Dutch Republic of the United Provinces 1579-1795

dr. Roel Pieterman

1 Introduction

As one compares Dutch history and developments within the European Union, striking parallels occur. Dutch developments in the 19th century constitute a period of change between what went on before, in the Republic, and what progressively came to be a unified State in the 19th century and more so in the 20th century.[1] Parallels with today's topic of flexibility, which refers to ideas of diversity, become very clear when one looks at the literature on the Dutch Republic, which many times has unity and diversity as a running theme. The first line of a dissertation by Marjolein 't Hart, *The making of the Bourgeois State, war, politics and finance during the Dutch revolt*, illustrates the parallels perfectly:

> *'From the early beginnings of the new born state, disparity and discord were to rule the Netherlands provinces, which united against Spain.'*

Putting disparity, discord and unison all in one sentence sums up very nicely what the Dutch Republic means.

The present contribution gives a short analysis of several points on which a comparison with the European Union can be made. However, detailed comparisons are not made. The emphasis remains on the Dutch Republic.

2 Need for unity and interest in diversity

Where for the EC there was a political and an economic origin or need for unity, in 1579 the Dutch need for unity was political and military in nature. This did not change for the next two centuries, because after the struggle for independence with Spain that ended in 1648, Europe remained a 'theatre of war'. Unity however was not a goal in itself, but merely a means to an end. Paradoxically, the end was to retain sovereignty for each province, and to retain their sovereignty, the provinces needed to unite. This was a very problematic mix, which remained problematic; it was never solved through a real everyday political process. But it had to be solved at the end of the 18th century, through a revolutionary process.

What were the interests in diversity? The Dutch revolt against Spain was very much a struggle of provincial elite's, against royalist centralisation. Because the revolt was successful, the United Provinces were able to continue medieval

[1] R. Pieterman, *De plaats van de rechter in Nederland 1830-1920: politiek-juridische ideeënstrijd over de scheiding van machten in de staat*, Arnhem, 1990.

practices. These practices however, came to rule a novel situation. Instead of an equilibrium with a sovereign lord, who personified the unity, now the provincial states came in possession of sovereignty without any real unifying countervailing power. It would take until 1795 before an appeal for an integral, national unity could be expressed with any political clout.

3 Political unity

During the Dutch Republic, there was always a balance of unity and diversity. There were several bodies that gave form and substance to the unity, which also was called the Generality. These were the Estates General, the Council of State, the Stadholderate and the Admiralty. None of these, however, were able to break provincial sovereignty. Decisions in the Estates General required unanimity, and as delegates the members could not vote unless they had specific instructions from their provincial estates. Twice the Estates General tried to force a province into compliance with established policies. Once they failed, against Zeeland, and once they were successful, against Groningen. But the success was only in the short run. They quartered soldiers there, collected revenue, but as soon as the soldiers left, the provincial states of Groningen wrote to the Estate General saying: This caused so much havoc and harm that we will not be able to pay our dues to the Republic for the next couple of years. Thus it happened and after that there was never any other attempt to force one of the provinces into compliance with general policy. Since then, the typical style of Dutch governance is that of *government by persuasion.*

In some situations the Stadholder came close to a dominant position, but he always remained dependent on an alliance with the Orange regent factions in the Provincial Estates. The dominant doctrine remained that the Stadholder was not the employee of the Generality, but of each of the Provincial Estates. There were situations were there was no Stadholder and situations were there were two or even three stadholders. So there was not a great unifying force. Of course in times of war – and there were lots of times of war – the balance of power changed in favour of the Stadholder. To make things even worse, from a perspective of unity, it was not only at the level of provinces that the provincial estates claimed their own sovereignty, but within the provinces the major cities and the major noblemen claimed their own sovereignty as well, and this claim was many times very successful. The most important province was the province of Holland where 18 cities had voting rights in the provincial estates and a policy was never adopted against the will or forced upon one of the cities.

4 Other forms of unity: military, legal and economic

Military unity existed only in times of crisis. The Admiralty, which had to provide the means for the fleet, was never established as one body. There were five admiralties, each managed differently with regional interests in mind. The Stadholder was not, as I mentioned, appointed by the Estates General but by every provincial estate. Troops were paid for with finances from the provinces, and this led to a very far-reaching influence on appointments, marching orders etcetera from the provinces. So even in times of crisis the level of unity in the military field was not so great.

Legal unity was absent. An attempt has been made to create a Court with jurisdiction over all Provinces but this never got beyond the establishment of a Supreme Court for the Provinces of Holland and Zeeland. As is almost always the case – and here the European Community is an important exception – legal jurisdiction did not reach further than political sovereignty. This rule applies also to the jurisdiction of provincial courts over the legal authorities in the major cities.

Economic and fiscal unity was hardly present. Local currencies abounded. The differences between the commercial activity of Holland and Zeeland and the agricultural economy of the inland provinces broke the attempt at fiscal unity. There was an attempt earlier on, it came with a proposal to adopt the Holland system everywhere in the Republic, but because of the large economic differences the Holland system was not feasible in the other provinces.

5 Dominance within the Republic

In the Dutch Republic the Province Holland was by far the most dominant. For two centuries it paid for 55% or more of the budget of the Republic, where recent calculations indicate that this 55% was less than its proportion of the total Dutch economic affluence. Holland dominated, if not dictated, foreign policy and many times, even at a lower level, the city of Amsterdam had its own diplomatic agenda. This dominance led to the prevalence of military interest at sea over those on land; the fleet was always better equipped than the army. In times of need it was possible, and it was done once, to break certain dikes and to create an inland water defence for the Province of Holland.

However, during the two centuries of the Republic, the commercial economy gradually became somewhat less important relative to the agricultural economy of the inland provinces. This led to a certain shift in the balance of power in the Republic. However throughout this period Holland remained the dominant force. This still is represented in the fact that the name for our country, the Netherlands, is hardly used, and most of the time people refer to 'Holland'.

6 Attempts to more unity

Several attempts were made to have more unity. It is interesting to study them not only in their internal qualities but also in terms of a political struggle that led nowhere, until the end of the 18th century when the French marched into our country. And we had a revolution in which we had a body count of one and that seems to have been a mistake. Just before the French reached a city, the government was handed over to another faction, which was a beautiful Dutch way to have a revolution. Only after 1795 more appeals for an integral, national unity were successfully expressed. However, the time of indirect or direct French rule in the Netherlands (1795-1813) never led to a generally accepted vision of a united nation.

After 1813 several factors contributed to a political basis on which the Kingdom of the Netherlands could be built. There was the concept for a constitution by Van Hogendorp. There was political assertiveness of some prominent Amsterdam citizens. Some historians say that the formative event in the forming of a united kingdom took place at Dam square in Amsterdam, where Prince William VI became King William I. He was persuaded by some liberal citizens of Amsterdam to proclaim that he accepted the sovereignty for the Netherlands in front of the Amsterdam populace. This was done to prevent the old powers from reclaiming their sovereignty after this revolutionary event. So this was a major factor contributing to more unity, as was the person of King William I himself. Last but not least, and maybe the most important, there was a pressure from the allied forces that again tried to force the Northern and the Southern Provinces into a political unity.

The struggle for provincial autonomy continued in the deliberations of the Constitutional Committee, headed by Van Hogendorp. The basic balance he envisaged was that between the King as a sovereign and the Second Chamber consisting of delegates of all Provincial Estates. As a member of the Second Chamber he later became very disillusioned about the fact that the provincial delegates hardly used their capacity for countervailing power.

In the southern part of the Netherlands there was a rebellion against the Dutch and an own State was created in the summer of 1830. In the Netherlands the struggle for unity continued. In the realm of law, for instance, provinces maintained a fair degree of autonomy through a system of provincial courts. It was only in 1875 that this system was abolished.

7 The context of greater unity

I would finally like to point out some conditions that led to this increased unity. Between 1579 and 1813, Europe saw the development of larger political bodies. In this environment the Netherlands had either to go along or become part of another state.

Within the Netherlands, there was a growing importance of an independent citizenry consisting of academically trained professionals and small but independent merchants and farmers. The oligarchic Regent families had to come to a new understanding with this group. As elsewhere the interplay of three social forces – monarchy, aristocracy and democracy – led to new and changing state formations. In these developments the bureaucratic element became ever more important. The development of a state bureaucracy provided new opportunities for members of the independent citizenry. It was in order to survive as an independent state that the Dutch had to do away with the Regents as a system of amateur rule.

8 Conclusions

From this brief historical sketch we can learn the following:

A political entity which is a unity in some respects and instances and full of discord in others can survive successfully for a long time by 'going with the flow' of international events. Overcoming discord and achieving unity usually comes as a result of external pressures. It must be remembered that formal results always have to be given substance and endurance in concrete practices.

CHAPTER III

Flexibility in German Constitutional Law

prof. dr. Gerard van Wissen

1 Introduction

In the ECSA Newsletter written by Stubb the institutionalisation of flexible integration, introduced in the Amsterdam Treaty, is defined as 'the possibility for a number of Member States to cooperate more closely in specific areas using the institutional framework of the Union'.[1] This definition will be the starting point of my attempt to provide a short survey of the possibilities of flexible cooperation – of flexibility – within the German constitutional system. This paper discusses the extent and the legal and constitutional structure of cooperation between the constitutional institutions, that is between the Federation and the *Länder* and between the *Länder* among themselves. Or, more precisely, with Stubb's definition of flexibility at hand: is there a possibility for the Federation and one or more *Länder* or for two or more *Länder*, to cooperate more closely in specific areas, using the institutional framework of the Federation?

2 The German federal model

Each federal model is different. In a very informing article on the division of competencies between Community and Member States, Geelhoed, at that time Secretary General of the Dutch Ministry of Economic Affairs, makes a useful distinction between two types of federalism: a *dualistic* model and a more *cooperative* one.[2] In a purely dualistic federal system the division of competencies between the federal institutions and the states is clear and transparent. That is important with respect to the responsibility of the institutions on the various levels and also for the democratic control on the activities of these institutions. Geelhoed is not very positive about the cooperative model in this respect. Especially if cooperation between the institutions based on contract or agreement is possible, it creates, so he fears, an obscure and non-transparent situation. Questions about what decisions have been made, who is responsible for them, and so on, remain unanswered. Democratic control by the parliament is difficult; a kind of technocratic coloured '*Politikverflechtung*' can easily develop. Germany is a clear example of the cooperative model. Between the Federation and the *Länder* on the one hand and among the *Länder* on the other, there are two kinds of cooperation: (a) the cooperation based on the *constitution* and (b) the cooperation primarily based on *agreement*.

---

1 A.C-G. Stubb, "The Amsterdam Treaty and Flexible Integration", *ECSA Newsletter*, Spring 1988.

2 L.A. Geelhoed, "Competentieperikelen: De bevoegdhedenverdeling tussen de Gemeenschap en de Lid-Staten in het licht van de evolutie van het Europese integratieproces", in H.J. de Ru and J. A. Hofman (eds.), *Nieuw Europees Constitutioneel Recht*, Nijmegen, 1992, p. 82-101.

3 Cooperation based on the Constitution

In many respects the German constitution, the *Grundgesetz* (Basic Law; BL), regulates and enables the cooperation between Federation and *Länder*. The following examples make this clear:

a) The *Bundesrat*, through which the *Länder* participate in the legislative process and administration and in matters concerning the European Union (Article 50 BL) enables cooperation between *Länder*. The subject of European integration is more in detail regulated in Article 23 BL, which links the internal responsibility of the *Länder*, their interests and especially their legislative powers to the right to participate through the *Bundesrat*.[3]
b) The *Länder* implement federal legislation in their own right in so far as the Basic Law does nor provide or permit otherwise (Article 83 BL). Article 84 BL contains the implementation by the *Länder* under supervision by the Federal Government and Article 85 BL regulates the implementation by the *Länder* for the Federation.
c) The administration of justice gives an example of this cooperation as well. Federal courts and the courts of the *Länder* are linked with each other to one administration of justice.
d) A clear example of constitutional possibilities of cooperation between Federation and *Länder* provides chapter VIIIa, called 'Joint Responsibilities' (*Gemeinschaftsaufgaben*). As Article 91 (a) (1) BL says: 'The Federation shall participate in discharging the responsibilities of the Länder in the following areas provided that they are relevant to the community as a whole and that its participation is necessary in order to improve living conditions' .
e) The constitutional system of legislation provides a clear and well-known example of this cooperation. Article 70 BL provides as follows: '(1) The Länder have the right to legislate in so far as this Basic Law does not confer legislative powers on the Federation. (2) The legislative jurisdiction of the Federation and the Länder shall be governed by the provisions of this Basic Law concerning exclusive and concurrent legislation.'

The constitution deals mostly with cooperation between Federation and the *Länder*. This is only logical, because in a federal system the federal constitution,

[3] Art. 23, par. 6 BL provides as follows: 'Where essentially the exclusive legislative jurisdiction of the *Länder* is affected the exercise of the rights of the Federal Republic of Germany as a member state of the European Union shall be transferred by the Federation to a representative of the *Länder* designated by the *Bundesrat*. Those rights shall be exercised with the participation of and made in agreement with the Federal Government; in this connection the responsibility of the Federation for the country as a whole shall be maintained.'

such as the German *Grundgesetz*, provides primarily the federal rules and federal institutions. Nevertheless some regulations in the *Grundgesetz* affect the relation among the *Länder* themselves. Thus Article 32 par. 3 BL enables the *Länder*, with the consent of the Federal Government, to conclude treaties, not only with each other, but also with other countries.[4] Another example of intra-*Länder* cooperation based on the constitution is the financial equalisation (*Finanzausgleich*). Indeed, Article 106 BL deals with the so-called 'vertical financial equalisation' (*vertikaler Finanzausgleich*), *i.e.* the division of tax revenues between Federation and *Länder*, but there is a horizontal financial equalisation as well. Article 107, par. 2 BL prevents differences in financial respect between the *Länder* to become too great. Both types of financial equalisation are to be realised by a federal law. So richer *Länder* like Baden-Wurtemberg and Hessen have to pay for the poorer ones, which include all the new *Länder* in the former German Democratic Republic.

I do not believe that the cooperation based on the constitution will entail the dangers of obscurity and non-transparency, which Geelhoed fears in a cooperative system. Although in the past there were some problems with the 'joint responsibilities' (*Gemeinschaftsaufgaben*), Article 91 (a) BL now contains the procedures to follow and the financial responsibilities of Federation and *Länder*.[5] That is probably different with respect to the other type of cooperation, namely the cooperation by agreement.

4 Cooperation based on agreement

This kind of cooperation is usually called *the flexible co-ordination and cooperation*. One can make a distinction between horizontal and vertical flexible cooperation.

The *vertical flexible cooperation* is between Federation and *Länder*. For example, they can create together common institutions like the *Hochschule für Verwaltungswissenschaften* in Speyer and the *Richterakademie* in Trier. Article 91 (b) BL deals with this kind of cooperation:

> *'The Federation and the* Länder *may, pursuant to agreements, cooperate in educational planning and in the promotion of research institutions and projects of supra-regional importance. The apportionment of costs shall be regulated by the relevant agreements.'*

---

4 Subjects dealt with include tourist information of the *Länder* abroad (*Ambtliche Bayerische Reisebüro*), creation of joint nature conservation areas, environmental management of transboundary river basins.

5 It meant a transition from an intensive co-ordination of the relations between Federation and *Länder* towards a common fulfilment of obligations.

In contrast with Article 91 (a) BL neither a procedure is prescribed in Article 91 (b) BL nor are the financial consequences settled. The article is open and does not provide a clear frame like the constitutional provisions do, as mentioned above. An agreement between Federation and *Länder* has to realise the cooperation in all its aspects. The *Bundesverfassungsgericht* (Federal Constitutional Court) has warned several times that these agreements should not affect the interests of the non participating *Länder.* Due to the strong position of the Federation the position of the participating *Länder* is not safeguarded in these agreements. In this context, Geelhoed may be right that this cooperation contains certain risks.

The *horizontal flexible cooperation* is between two or more *Länder. Länder* are entitled to conclude treaties with each other (*Staatsverträge*).[6] They can establish joint institutions, for example ZDF in Mayence. There can be joint decisions (*Beschlüsse*) and agreements (*Verwaltungsabkommen*), frequently taken by or arranged at the periodical conferences of the Prime Ministers and Ministers of the *Länder.* Article 91 (b) BL provides a – not very concise – constitutional base for agreements between Federation and two or more *Länder,* but a constitutional base for horizontal flexible cooperation fails. The *Länder* may cooperate with each other as far as they stay within their competencies. They may affect neither the interests of the Federation nor those of the non-participating *Länder.*

The conclusion of treaties goes on by an established legal procedure. The conclusion of agreements and decisions, however, is often not so transparent, and democratic control by the *Landtag,* the parliament of the Land, as a consequence, is usually very difficult. It is important to mention that similar problems can arise in a unitary state. The Netherlands is a unitary state, but with a cooperative model. Complaints about transparency and democratic control are often heard with regard to regulations based on 'The law on joint regulations' (*Wet gemeenschappelijke regelingen*). One may conclude that problems are caused primarily by the cooperative model, more so than by the fact that the country in question is a federation.

5 Centralisation

Germany has been a federation for more than a century and in that century there has been a strong tendency to centralisation, notwithstanding its federal character. What was the reason of that development?

6 *E.g.* Article 29, par. 7 BL states that certain modifications of Land boundaries may be effected by agreement between the *Länder* concerned. Conclusion of treaties between *Länder* involves approval of their parliaments, according to the procedure prescribed by their domestic law.

In 1871 the German Empire was proclaimed. It was a federation, not a confederation like the previous German League but an alliance of states with a very different character, with Bavaria on the one hand and Prussia on the other. The first aim of the federation was to shape one Germany and to turn the Bavarians, Prussians, Saxonians and so on into Germans. '*Sei einig, einig, einig!*' was printed on German stamps at the end of the century and in the German national anthem was sung '*Einigkeit und Recht und Freiheit für das Deutsche Vaterland*', with '*Einigkeit*' as the first and most important wish for the newly founded empire. Centralisation was the consequence, notwithstanding the formal strong constitutional position of the states. I realise that every situation is different and the position of Germany at the end of the 19th century cannot be compared with the situation in Germany or Europe nowadays. Nevertheless I dare to put forward the proposition that there usually is a strong tendency in newly formed federations to centralise powers and competencies. A new federation creates many new opportunities for its people. There are new possibilities for trade, scientific exchange etc. Many people go to other, richer parts of the federation, looking for better living conditions. All this makes more federal regulations desirable and sometimes even necessary.

Since 1934 Nazi Germany was not only *de facto*, but also *de jure* a unitary state. That is no surprise: dictatorial states and federal systems do not go together. In 1952 the German Democratic Republic repealed officially the federal system and the Soviet Union was, in spite of its name, as a matter of fact, no federation at all.

In post-war Germany the federal system was restored, partially under strong pressure of the Allied Powers. The central article in the Basic Law is Article 30:

> '*Except as otherwise provided or permitted by this Basic Law the exercise of governmental powers and the discharge of governmental functions shall be incumbent on the* Länder.'

Paragraph 1 of Article 70 BL gives a presumption of legislative powers in favour of the *Länder*:

> 'The Länder *have the right to legislate in so far as this Basic Law does not confer legislative powers on the Federation*'.

The federal system chosen was a very cooperative one, as we have seen. An example of that cooperative character is the possibility of *concurrent legislation* given in Article 72 BL:

> '(1) *In matters of concurrent legislation the* Länder *have the right to legislate as long and to the extent that the Federation does not exercise its legislative powers.*

(2) *The Federation has the right to legislate where*
1. a matter cannot be effectively regulated by the legislation of individual Länder*, or*
2. regulation by a Land *might prejudice the interests of other* Länder *or the country as a whole or*
3. the maintenance of legal and economic unity, especially uniform living conditions beyond the territory of any one Land*, calls for federal legislation'.*

It is important to notice that with regard to this concurrent legislation there is also a presumption of law in favour of the *Länder.*

However, reality was different. Article 73 BL (exclusive federal powers) was permanently widened. One can think of several reasons for the tendency to centralise. Thus, Germany is a large country, but on world scale it belongs to the larger middle-sized countries. Therefore different legislation on important matters within such a country is not very convenient and this fact easily tends to centralisation. In such a middle-sized country 16 *Länder* are too large a number. The cities Berlin, Hamburg and Bremen are *Länder* on their own and several *Länder* are small and weak. Especially the maintenance of uniform living conditions beyond the territory of any one Land, as mentioned in Article 72 and Article 91 (a) BL, requires federal legislation. It is the consequence of the idea of the 'Welfare State', a state that cares for the well-being of its citizens, that cannot accept that the differences become too big among the *Länder* concerning the living conditions of their citizens.

6 Present position of the Länder

There was not only a strong centralisation in Germany since 1949, but a strong movement towards uniformity as well and consequently a weakening of the position of the *Länder* in many respects. In response, the *Länder* strongly defend their remaining competencies, especially in the *Bundesrat*, where they can block the legislative process, forcing the federal government to concessions. Another example of *Länder* defending their position is that every *Land* has its 'embassy' in Brussels to take care of its own interests. Therefore it is not always easy for Germany to speak with one voice in Brussels.

An interesting kind of horizontal flexible cooperation concludes this survey. Several so-called 'old' *Länder* cooperate with 'new' *Länder* to help them build a modern *Land.* They help to build a well-functioning administration and to actualise all the regulations a *Land* has to bring in force. So Hessen helps Thuringia and Bavaria supports Saxonia. Perhaps the idea of such a partnership can be an interesting example for the coming enlargement of Europe with Eastern European states.

CHAPTER IV

Switzerland: From Confederation to Federation Through Flexibility

dr. Flora Goudappel

1 Introduction

The *Confederatio Helvetica*, as the country is officially named in its federal Constitution,[1] is the most prominent example of a federal form of government which was allowed to be created and was able to grow because of flexibility. Nowadays, several forms of enhanced cooperation, as the official EU-label is named, are still present in the Swiss constitutional system. For this study, flexibility will be considered to indicate a system in which it is possible for one or preferably more Cantons to go one step further in legislation than the federation as a whole goes. Thus, flexibility is not represented by a list of cases in which the Cantons have exclusive powers opposite the Confederation (powers which have remained in the hands of the Cantons with which the Confederation has nothing to do), but rather by the possibilities for at least several Cantons to move ahead of the Confederation in policy and legislation.

In this study, flexibility will be discussed as it has appeared in the past and as it appears nowadays in the Swiss federal system. First, several borderline cases need to be discussed. Do they represent flexibility or not? Secondly, the flexible history of Switzerland will be discussed. After this, several prominent examples of flexibility in the present-day system will be described.

2 Borderline cases

The definition of flexibility given above leaves us with several borderline cases, for which it is not clear in which category they fall: are they flexible or rather autonomous? They all result from an important historical aspect of the Swiss constitutional system, namely from the fact that it is a centripetal federal system, originating from independent units which move and have moved towards a central point. The constitutional result is that the Confederate Constitution concentrates on powers given to the Confederation while only mentioning the powers in the hands of the Cantons when they form an exception to a power attributed to the Confederation. All powers not mentioned in the Confederate Constitution, have remained in the hands of the Cantons.

A prominent example of these borderline cases is the right to grant citizenship. Article 43 sub 1 of the Confederate Constitution implies that the Cantons have the right to grant citizenship while the Confederation gives Confederate citizenship to anyone who has obtained Cantonal citizenship. The result of

---

1 Despite the implications of the name *Confederatio Helvetica*, this country is a federation and not a confederation (it is the Federal Constitution of the Swiss Confederation).

this system is that the Cantons are free to choose their own requirements for citizenship, which could be more strict in one Canton opposite the other. Another prominent example can be found in the Cantonal constitutions. Article 6 of the Confederate Constitution only prescribes general limitations for the Cantons that are free to create their own constitutions within these (democratic) limitations. However, these examples do not reflect a form of closer cooperation between several Cantons but rather a way for each Canton individually to move faster than the Confederation as a whole.

The last group of borderline cases can be found in the functioning of the system of so-called horizontal cooperative federalism, *i.e.* the cooperation between Cantons within the federal system. Two kinds of horizontal cooperative federalism exist in Switzerland. The first one, the one in which Cantons are allowed to conclude a kind of treaty among themselves (*Vereinbarungen*), will be discussed at the end of this study. The second type, however, shows another borderline case when one considers whether it represents flexibility in the European sense. These '*interkantonale Konferenzen*' are formed by representatives of the governments of the Cantons and are institutionalised although they have been formed voluntarily. All Cantons participate in such conferences and they all have to agree on decisions, which are always taken in the policy fields of which the powers have remained in the hands of the Cantons.[2] Whether such arrangements can be considered to represent closer cooperation, remains a question since they only concern Cantonal powers and since it concerns all Cantons simultaneously.

3 Flexibility in history

The modern Swiss Confederation originates from a system of treaties on different subjects concluded between different Cantons in the Middle Ages. The first one was a pact between Uri, Schwytz and Unterwald in 1291, on what we would call nowadays a common defence system. Over the centuries, several other Cantons joined this confederate structure, and several other treaties were concluded, on different subjects (such as freedom of trade and military politics) and between different Cantons. An eye-catching example of this last instance is the *Pfaffenbrief* of 1370, which constituted the Confederation and which was concluded between six out of the seven Cantons then in alliance; Bern did not join this Confederation at the time. Thus, a system of flexibility existed between the Cantons in a manner which allowed several of them to go one step further in cooperation while the other Cantons did not

[2] U. Häfelin & W. Haller, *Schweizerisches Bundesstaatsrecht; Ein Grundruss*, Zürich, 1993, p. 150.

have any obligation to join the new treaty immediately. Simultaneously, the fact that one or more Cantons did not want to join, did not stop the others from joining.[3]

4 Flexibility in the present day constitutional system

In the modern Swiss federal system, the notion of 'flexibility' is hardly mentioned in literature or legislation; 'autonomy' is used more regularly. When flexibility in the European sense is mentioned in literature, it often has a negative connotation, connecting it with inequality and a lack of clarity of political relations.[4] In general, a movement towards unification of the federal system can be observed, which is the result of the century-old movement from confederation to federation. Closer cooperation is therefore only possible for the powers that the Confederate Constitution has left in the hands of the Cantons, not for the policy fields which have been attributed to the Confederation. This is in contrast with the system of flexibility in the European Union, which concerns powers which basically belong to the European Union but for which several Member States wish to move forward.

Thus, flexibility in the modern Swiss federal system mostly appears in the form of horizontal cooperative federalism in general, and in the *interkantonale Vereinbarungen* or *concordats* in specific. This has constitutionally been made possible in Article 7 of the Confederate Constitution, which sets some limits to closer cooperation. As can be expected, these limits mean that the contents of *concordats* between the Cantons cannot contradict Confederate policy or legislation (Article 7 sub 2), and that these *concordats* are not allowed to have a political content (Article 7 sub 1). Such forms of horizontal cooperative federalism can only be created in policy fields that are constitutionally in the hands of the Cantons. This means that, in contrast to the situation in the European Union, the cooperation is not connected to the policies of the Confederation but to the policies of the Cantons. It thus represents the relations between the Cantons. Still, two or more Cantons may go a few steps further forward than the others do.

Most of the *concordats* are concluded for geographical or economic reasons.[5] As a result, the *concordats* usually have a regional character or are part of regional external relations. In the latter case, it concerns only the part of external

---

3 E. Weibel, *Esquisse du fédalisme suisse. Son évolution historique et ses traits distinctifs* (conference paper), not published, 1989.

4 C. Wehrli, "Langlebigkeit des schweizerischen Föderalismus", in: A. Döpfner (ed.), *Keine Angst vor Europa. Föderalismus als Chance*, Zürich, 1992, p. 120-133.

5 U. Häfelin & W. Haller, *Schweizerisches Bundesstaatsrecht; Ein Grundruss*, Zürich, 1993, p. 157-158.

relations which has remained in the hands of the Cantons.[6] The regional cooperation (sometimes referred to as 'microfederalism'[7]) appears to concentrate on public transport and traffic, such as regional railway connections and highway police.[8] The regional external relations concentrate, for instance, on different subjects for the Italian-speaking Canton of Ticino, or on the incorporation of Liechtenstein in several regional Swiss schemes. In addition, several intercantonal institutions have been created, for instance in order to check fishing agreements about a lake or river.[9]

Finally, there are several *concordats* that fall more outside the scope of true flexibility since they are meant to create uniformity in law between the Cantons without transferring a power to the Confederation. These mostly concern education and taxes.

5 Concluding remarks

In conclusion has to be observed that the history of Switzerland shows that the Confederation was built and changed into a federal structure by means of flexibility. Originally, treaties were closed between different Cantons, which finally led to a closely-knit confederate system. This tradition is more or less continued in the modern Swiss federal system. The Cantons still conclude agreements amongst themselves on different subjects, although the Confederate Constitution does not leave many powers exclusively in the hands of the Cantons,[10] powers which represent policy fields in which intercantonal *concordats* may be concluded.

It can thus be observed that the Swiss experience with flexibility apparently shows that closer cooperation is a necessary means for a new pre-federal structure to grow towards a closer integration. Later on, only relatively unimportant forms of closer cooperation need to exist because the function of flexibility has become more and more obsolete since it was taken over by a strong federal structure in which the states (*in casu* the Cantons) still have a say in the decisions taken at the highest level.

---

6 See F.A.N.J. Goudappel, *Powers and Control Mechanisms in European Federal Systems*, Deventer, 1997, p. 50-51.

7 R. Friedrich, "Kräftespiel im Mikroföderalismus; Das Tessin und seine 'Aussenpolitik'", in: A. Döpfner (ed.), *Keine Angst vor Europa. Föderalismus als Chance*, Zürich, 1992, p. 69-80.

8 Examples: the agreement between St. Gallen, Schwyz and Zürich on the building of roads/highways; or the agreement between Thurgau and Zürich on the highway police for the N1 and the N7.

9 For instance, the agreement between Zürich, Schwyz, Glarus and St. Gallen about fishing on Lake Zürich, the Linth Channel, and Lake Walen, has created a Fishing Commission.

10 F.A.N.J. Goudappel, *Powers and Control Mechanisms in European Federal Systems*, Deventer, 1997, p. 47-49.

CHAPTER V

The Ubiquity of Asymmetrical Government

Some Constitutional and International Experiences

prof. dr. Bruno de Witte

1 Introduction

The decision, reflected in the Treaties of Amsterdam and Nice, to create arrangements for more flexible relations between the member states of the European Union is less unusual, and therefore less alarming, than one may think. It is true that, in Community law, there has traditionally been a strong ethos of uniformity, encouraged also by the jurisprudence of the European Court of Justice. Although the idea that the relations between the member states and the Union, or between the member states horizontally, should not be perfectly symmetrical may seem rather novel within the EU context, it actually corresponds to a widespread reality in the constitutional law of European states, and also, albeit in a different way, in the international relations of those European states. I propose therefore to make a brief excursion into constitutional law and international law in order to situate the developments of EU law in the wider perspective of trends occurring in these two other fields of law, starting with constitutional law.

Legal *diversity* is inherent in the existence of federal or quasi-federal government, because the autonomy given to sub-national governments implies that those governments may adopt rules and policies that differ from each other. Flexibility, or *asymmetry*, is an additional feature that is not inherent in federal government. It means, for the purpose of this paper, that the institutions or powers of the various sub-national units are not identical, or that the relations between these units and the central government do not run along the same lines. Although, theoretically speaking, a perfectly symmetrical federal system would seem more stable than an asymmetrical one,[1] the reality of most federal or quasi-federal systems shows an extensive degree of flexibility and asymmetry. The recent devolution of powers to Scotland and Wales and also, but in a different context, to Northern Ireland, is strikingly asymmetrical, as no arrangements for regional government are provided for the English part of the UK. The concern expressed about this selective regionalisation has been countered, in the literature, by pointing to the fact that some degree of asymmetry is to be found in most states with a federal or regional government.[2]

---

1 See the abstract model proposed by C.D. Tarleton, "Symmetry and Asymmetry as Elements of Federalism: A Theoretical Speculation", *Journal of Politics*, 1965, p. 861.

2 See M. Keating, "What's Wrong with Asymmetrical Government?", *Regional and Federal Studies*, 1998, p. 195; for a comparative survey of the asymmetrical features of current federal and regional systems, see E. Fossas Espadaler, "Autonomía y asimetría", *Informe Pi i Sunyer sobre Comunidades Autónomas 1994*, Barcelona, 1995, p. 890.

2 Spain and Belgium

The most striking examples of this, in today's Western Europe, are Spain and Belgium. In the categories used by constitutional lawyers, Belgium and Spain do not quite fit within the same box. Since 1993, Belgium is affirmed to be, in the words of Article 1 of its Constitution, a federal State. The Spanish Constitution does not use the word 'federal'. Indeed, Spain is declared, by the Constitution, to be a unified state. But that state is divided in autonomous communities *(comunidades autónomas)* which resemble member states of a federation, as they have autonomous legislative powers in a broad range of policy areas and benefit from constitutional protection for their powers, in the form of the judicial control by the Spanish Constitutional Court. Still, the term 'Federation' is not used; instead, Spain is described as a 'regional state' or simply, and in a somewhat tautological way, as a 'State of the Autonomies' (*Estado de las Autonomías*), which is the official expression used in Spain. But whether or not Spain should be termed federal, quasi-federal or federal-in-the-making[3], the fact remains that Belgium and Spain have a number of common constitutional features: there is a division of legislative powers between two levels of government; this has occurred through a devolution of powers from the centre to the periphery; and the decisive motive and driving force for this was the political salience of both countries' cultural diversity. It is this same cultural, or linguistic, diversity which accounts for the asymmetrical features of those two systems, which I am now turning to.

A peculiar characteristic of regional government in Spain is that the Constitution of 1978, which is still in force and almost unchanged today, does not contain a list of the Autonomous Communities. Indeed, the idea inspiring the drafters of the Constitution was, like John Major's ideas for the European Union, that of a sort of *à la carte* devolution of powers. There was no fixed list of sub-national units, and there was no fixed list of competencies that those units would have. What one does find in the text of the Constitution, however, is a distinction between two different types of component units of the Spanish state, namely *nacionalidades* and *regiones*. This was the recognition of the basic political reality at the time of transition to democracy, that in many areas of the country, like Castilia, there was no particular aspiration to regional autonomy, whilst there was a very strong regionalist movement in what were called, and are still called, the *historical communities* (or *nationalities*, to use the constitutional expression), namely the Basque Country, Catalonia and Galicia.

---

[3] M. Guibernau, "Spain: A Federation in the Making?", in G. Smith (ed), *Federalism: The Multiethnic Challenge*, London, 1995, p. 239.

It is true that the *nacionalidades* and *regiones* were given the same institutional form, that of Autonomous Communities, and in fact the whole country was soon divided in such Autonomous Communities. Yet, behind this apparent symmetry, very different realities exist. If one examines the way legislative powers are allocated by the Spanish Constitution, one finds two lists: a first list of powers reserved to the central State, including fields such as foreign affairs and defence, and a second list of powers which may be exercised by the 'ordinary' Autonomous Communities. But the Autonomous Communities 'of the first rank' are entitled to exercise further powers, with the upper limit being the powers reserved to the central State. In other words, the two lists in the Constitution leave a gap between them, and this gap may be filled only by the most prominent Autonomous Communities through an assumption of the powers not listed in the Constitution. The first rank, that of the Autonomous Communities with a large degree of autonomy, is occupied by five of them, namely the Basque Country, Catalonia, Galicia, Navarra and Andalucia. Then there are two Autonomous Communities that have nearly but not quite the same degree of autonomy, namely Valencia and the Canary Islands. And finally, the ten remaining Communities occupy the third rank. Those within this third rank have basically the same structure and the same competencies, so that the extreme '*à la carte*' flexibility promised by the Spanish Constitution is no longer there. The distinction between *categories* of Communities, however, is strongly entrenched,[4] and is further accentuated by a political factor, namely the fact that the historical communities have their own political parties and that for several years now the successive Spanish governments have needed the support of regionalist parties in order to have a majority on their side in the national parliament. This fact obviously provides those parties, and through them the Communities which they represent, a strong influence on central state policies, which the other Autonomous Communities can only dream of.

Belgium has a different variety of asymmetrical federalism whose main characteristic is that it contains two different sets of member states with overlapping territories, namely the three Communities and the three Regions. Both the Communities and the Regions have legislative powers, albeit in different fields: education, cultural and social services for the Communities, economic policies and environmental protection for the Regions. The three Communities are the Flemish Community, the French Community, and the German-speaking Community, whereas the three Regions are Flanders, Wallonia and Brussels. Because of the incomplete territorial overlap between these two sets of governments, two persons living in different towns in Belgium can be part of the same

[4] For a general assessment, see E. Aja Fernández, "La dimensión constitucional del hecho diferencial en el Estado autonómico", *Anuario de Derecho Constitucional y Parlamentario*, 1996, p. 157.

Region but of a different Community, or the other way round. For instance, persons living in Liège and Eupen belong to the same Region, Wallonia, but they belong to two different Communities: the person in Liège is part of the French-speaking Community, and the person living in Eupen of the German-speaking Community. Similarly, two Dutch-speaking persons, one of them living in Brussels and the other in Antwerp, belong to the same Community, the Flemish Community, but to two different regions, Brussels and Flanders.

This unique feature of Belgian federalism is compounded by further elements of asymmetry, particularly the fact that the three Communities do not have identical powers, nor do the three Regions. The German-speaking Community has fewer competencies than its two bigger counterparts, and the Brussels Region possesses a lesser degree of autonomy than the Flemish and Walloon Regions.

There is a third level of asymmetry in the Belgian institutional framework, in that the Flemish Region and the Flemish Community have set up common institutions (there is one single Flemish government, dealing with regional and community matters, and one single Flemish assembly), whereas on the other, French-speaking side of the main linguistic divide, separate institutions continue to serve the Walloon Region and the French Community.[5]

Now, despite what may appear at first glance, these are not gratuitous complications. Like everywhere else, constitutional flexibility was introduced in such massive doses, not because the Belgian citizens particularly like those complications but because of political necessity. This particular pattern of flexibility is directly linked to the linguistic diversity in the country and the way in which the different linguistic communities are distributed over its territory. Yet, the cumbersome institutional structure certainly has not helped the Belgian federal state to attract the loyal support of its citizens.

So, both in Spain and in Belgium, the normal degree of diversity which is inherent in federalism or in regional government, and which one finds also in countries like Germany or the United States, is much more accentuated. Not only is there a differentiation among the sub-national units in which these countries are divided, but they also have a weak system of horizontal cooperation between those units, as compared to, say, Germany, where horizontal cooperation between the *Länder* is a powerful unifying force. In Belgium, the possibility of such horizontal cooperation between the Regions, or between the Communities, is provided by the Constitution, but is not actively used due to the mistrust between the partners, whereas in Spain horizontal cooperation has, so far, been rather discouraged by the central government and by the Constitutional Court.

---

[5] For a synthetic view, see V. Bartholomée, "L'asymétrie", in F. Delpérée (ed), *La Belgique fédérale*, Brussels, 1994, p. 61.

3 France

It appears, from the foregoing observations, that flexibility is not a feature which all federal systems possess in identical doses. On the other hand, one can also observe unsuspected degrees of flexibility in countries renowned for their unitary and symmetrical institutional tradition. A case in point is that of France. This country is the historical model of symmetry and uniformity, and its institutional ethos is adequately symbolised by the lay-out *à la française* of the royal park in Versailles. So, France may well be divided into regions, departments and local communities, but all the single units, within each category, are expected to have identical powers and organs and have the same type of relationship with Paris. The expectation is, in other words, that the state's power should be exercised in the same way throughout the national territory. The messy constitutional reality is increasingly far removed from that model. The principle of the unity and the indivisible nature of the state is solemnly proclaimed in Article 2 of the Constitution, but that Article has been given a rather pluralist reading in recent legislative and judicial practice.[6] The Constitution itself has, for a long time already, allowed for the creation of territories with a special legal regime: the TOM or *territoires d'outre mer,* each of which has its own very specific system which is different from the next. Polynésie, Nouvelle Calédonie, St. Pierre-et-Miquelon, and Wallis-et-Futuna all have their own organisation and their own competencies, differing from each other and from the 'mainland' model. The most extreme example of flexibility within the bounds of the French Constitution is the agreement on the future status of New Caledonia, concluded on 21 April 1998, in which France recognised that this territory will move towards a kind of semi-sovereign state, which will have all the characteristics of an independent country, although the word '*indépendance*' itself is not actually used.[7]

Leaving apart these overseas territories, France nowadays offers another interesting example of constitutional differentiation closer to Paris, namely Corsica. This is not (or no longer) a *région* like the other, but rather a territorial unit *sui generis.* The scope of its autonomous powers is broader than that of the ordinary regions, it has its own set of institutions (there is, for instance, an *Assemblée de Corse,* whereas the other regions have to be content with a

---

6 A synthetic view is provided by C. Grewe, "L'unité de l´Etat: entre indivisibilité et pluralisme", *Revue du droit public* , 1998, p. 1349; for a more detailed analysis, see R. Debbasch, "L'indivisibilité de la République et l'existence de statuts particuliers en France", *Revue française de droit constitutionnel,* 1997, p. 359.

7 See the definition proposed in the title of a commentary on the agreement: J.-Y. Faberon, "La Nouvelle-Calédonie, pays à souveraineté partagée", *Revue du droit public,* 1998, p. 645.

Conseil régional) and its own electoral system. The elaboration of this special status for Corsica was contested before the *Conseil constitutionnel* some years ago, and interestingly, this constitutional court found that the highly particular legal regime for Corsica was compatible with the constitutional principle that the Republic should be, and remain, indivisible.[8] French commentators are of the opinion that, whereas the introduction of fully-fledged federalism throughout France would not be acceptable under the present Constitution, there are no objections any more against a fairly high degree of flexibility, provided that the main body of the system of territorial government looks somehow symmetrical and orderly.

The provisional conclusion is that, in matters of constitutional flexibility, there is no sharp divide between federal and unitary states, but rather a continuum. An analysis of the United Kingdom Constitution, both before and after the recent devolution reforms, would buttress this view. Yet, instead of that, I will now proceed to examine the other side of the institutional spectrum and point to some asymmetrical experiences in non-state political systems that are more loosely integrated than the European Union, namely the Commonwealth of Independent States and the Western European Union.

4 CIS and WEU

The Commonwealth of Independent States (CIS), the international organisation which acts as a partial successor to the former Soviet Union, is profoundly flexible and asymmetrical. Politically, it is clearly asymmetrical, because Russia is the dominant partner. Legally, the relationships among the Member States of the CIS have a different intensity and quality.[9] Within the framework of the CIS, hundreds of bilateral and multilateral treaties have been signed since the founding Treaty of Minsk was concluded in 1991. The parties to these treaties vary from case to case, in a manner which is reminiscent of the system of the Council of Europe: there is a general institutional framework within which a number of treaties have been adopted that can be signed by this or that country and not by the others. Beyond this *à la carte* character of

8 Decision of the *Conseil constitutionnel* of 9 May 1991; see the case comment by Th. Michalon, "La Corse entre décentralisation et autonomie. Vers la fin des catégories?", *Revue française de droit administratif*, 1991, p. 730 .

9 For more details, see S.V. Voitovich, "The Commonwealth of Independent States: An Emerging Institutional Model", *European Journal of International Law* , 1993, p. 403; J. Lippott, "The Commonwealth of Independent States as an Economic and Legal Community", *German Yearbook of International Law* 39, 1996, p. 334; Id., "Die Gemeinschaft Unabhängiger Staaten als einheitlicher Rechtsraum", *Zeitschrift für vergleichende Rechtswissenschaft* , 1998, p. 485.

the specific treaty commitments, a further asymmetry results from the fact that sub-organisations have been established within the CIS. A first sub-organisation is called the Commonwealth of Integrated States and is founded on a treaty concluded in 1996 between Russia, Belarus, Kazakhstan and Kirghistan. Within this sub-organisation, there is a further 'Russian doll', namely the even more integrated community set up between Russia and Belarus which might be moving, according to some observers, to the eventual creation of a (new) federal state. All these moves are compatible with the 'constitution' of the Commonwealth, which was precisely intended to allow its Member States the utmost flexibility without setting them any strict conditions.

The Western European Union (WEU) is a good example of a traditional international organisation with a high degree of variable geometry in its membership. States are associated to its activities in four different ways: there are ten full members (who are members of both the NATO and the European Union), there are six associate members who are within NATO but not within the EU (Iceland, Norway, Turkey, Czech Republic, Hungary and Poland), five observer States who are in the EU but not in NATO (Austria, Finland, Ireland, Denmark and Sweden) and ten associate partners (Central and Eastern European countries that are neither in NATO nor in the EU).[10] Variable geometry is therefore an essential characteristic of the WEU in its new capacity of providing the institutional 'bridge' between two organisations, NATO and EU, whose European membership does not coincide.

The asymmetrical features of the CIS and the WEU, though politically meaningful, are legally unremarkable, because they do, in fact, denote the ordinary flexible operation of international law under the thin veil of institutional order. Indeed, the flexible system *par excellence* is the international legal system, where relations between countries are established on an ad hoc basis, in the form of treaties. Each country is involved in a vast network of bilateral and multilateral treaties with almost every other country of the world, and no two networks are exactly the same. That was the situation in which Western European states found themselves before they created, or joined, the European Communities. And still today, it must not be forgotten, the relations between the fifteen member states of the European Union take place partly (and, no doubt, increas-

---

[10] After becoming members of the NATO, Hungary, the Czech Republic and Poland moved from the fourth to the second category. See A. Dumoulin and E. Remacle, *L'Union de l'Europe occidentale: Phénix de la défense européenne*, Brussels, 1998, particularly pages 351-354; and also, M. Weller, "The European Union within the 'European Security Architecture'", in M. Koskenniemi (ed), *International Law Aspects of the European Union*, The Hague, 1998, p. 57, at p. 65-66.

ingly) *within* the institutional context of the EU, but also partly *outside* that framework, on the basis of 'old-fashioned' international agreements.[11]

5 Conclusions

Looking at the recent developments in the European Union from this angle, one could conclude that the effort, made through the Treaties of Amsterdam and Nice, to set up clear rules on closer cooperation, was also, and above all, an effort at disciplining the relations between the member states of the Union, and at luring inside a system with guarantees of democratic control and transparency, initiatives that might otherwise take place outside the four corners of the European Union, in the vast and asymmetrical world of international law. In this respect, the *à la carte* model of the Commonwealth of Independent States is certainly not the model followed by the EU governments when adopting the Treaty of Amsterdam, and the European Union remains, comparatively speaking, a remarkably symmetrical and unitary institutional structure.

---

11 Among the areas in which bilateral agreements between member states continue to be used are trans-frontier cooperation, cultural and educational cooperation, conventions for the avoidance of double taxation, and agreements relating to common water resources.

CHAPTER VI

Flexibility in the American Context

dr. Timothy J. Conlan

1 Flexibility in the USA

A comment on the topic of flexibility in the United States should start with the observation that, outside of public administration, there is little use of this term in American political discourse. To be sure, the *concept* of flexibility is very important in the United States, not only from a legal and administrative perspective, but from the standpoint of political culture. The American approach to policy making is highly pragmatic, and that pragmatism encourages flexible arrangements between governmental units at all levels of the federal system. If there is an opportunity to 'do something' about a policy problem, politicians at every level of government are inclined to find a way to proceed. Nevertheless, political debates involving issues of flexibility have generally been conducted in the rhetoric of 'states rights' and 'devolution', rather than 'flexibility'.

This semantic distinction underscores important differences between our two political systems. In Europe, ultimate sovereignty still resides with the nation states that are parties to the various treaties that have led to European Union. Although these member states have surrendered a growing list of important powers to the community at large, they retain far more authority to negotiate opt outs and special arrangements than do American state governments. The concept of forming a core group of states in the US to advance the process of integration is entirely foreign, for example. Under the US Constitution, American states surrendered their sovereignty to the nation as a whole. Any doubts about this, or lingering thoughts of 'opting out' of national policy were ended by the Civil War. As the Supreme Court declared in *Texas v. White*[1], the United States is 'an indestructible Union, composed of indestructible states.'

2 Pragmatic flexibility

Despite their loss of sovereignty, the states retained many powers under the US Constitution, and these residual powers provide scope for many forms of interstate cooperation and flexibility. Article 11 of the Amsterdam version of the EC Treaty lists five conditions for flexible cooperation within the communities,[2] and these conditions would be a fair summation of the types of

---

1 *Texas v. White*, 7 Wallace 700, 74 U.S. 700 (1869).

2 The cooperation proposed: (a) does not concern areas which fall within the exclusive competence of the Community; (b) does not affect Community policies, actions or programmes; (c) does not concern the citizenship of the Union or discriminate between nationals of Member States; (d) remains within the limits of the powers conferred upon the Community by this Treaty; and (e) does not constitute a discrimination or a restriction of trade between Member States and does not distort the conditions of competition between the latter.

areas where US states are able to co-ordinate among themselves. Let me give you a few examples. Essentially what we are talking about are cases in which states are dealing with powers and functions that have been retained by them under the Constitution – functions that were not transferred to the national government. Such situations permit what John Shannon calls 'fend-for-yourself-federalism.'[3] Co-ordination often does occur, and it even extends to the local governmental level.

In the Washington D.C. region, for example, local government in the states of Maryland and Virginia plus the District of Columbia have formed special districts to deal with metropolitan transportation, sewage disposal, and drinking water issues. They are collaborating and co-ordinating freely in areas that do not affect other jurisdictions. Legally binding agreements between the different local governments have been sanctioned by the two States.

States themselves form inter-state compacts in areas that they are jointly interested in, such as flood control and water allocation within river basins.[4] This is an important issue in the US because, unlike most European countries, states boundaries were often carved out in abstract form by people far away looking at a map and trying to decide: 'where should we make a border?' Rivers provided natural borderlines, so they were often used to divide states. These are boundaries which make sense when you are map-making, but they make no sense from a functional perspective. Imagine the need for co-ordination if the border between Belgium and the Netherlands were the Rhine or the Maas rivers. It would create an obviously complex situation in cities like Rotterdam that would not represent the economic unity of the river basin.

For such reasons, American states come together to co-ordinate many ordinary things. They have both formal and informal structures for doing so, including conferences of state governments that meet regularly to collaborate on issues of State policy among different groups of states.

3 Sanctioned flexibility

The most interesting cases involving flexible collaboration are those that have been deliberately sanctioned by the national government. Such cases are particularly prominent in the field of environmental protection. One noteworthy example is the Clean Air Act. This is the basic statute regulating

---

[3] J. Shannon, "The Return of Fend-for-Yourself Federalism: The Reagan Marks," *Intergovernmental Perspective* 13, Summer-Fall 1987, p. 34-37.

[4] For an excellent study of this process, see M. Derthick, *Between State and Nation: Regional Organizations of the United States*, Washington, 1973.

air pollution in the United States, including tail pipe emissions from cars (and, in the US, anything affecting automobiles is *really* important), toxic and other airborne emissions from industries, and so on.

The way in which the Clean Air Act and many other health and safety laws are formulated is that they establish a uniform minimum standard that applies nation-wide. All states and metropolitan areas must meet certain standard air quality levels for different kinds of air pollution. But – and this is where flexibility comes in – the states can adopt more stringent regulations if they wish.[5] They are given free licence under federal law to adopt more potent pollution control standards. And they have done so on both an individual basis and on a joint or collaborative basis. The most famous case involves California. Cars have to be built with special exhaust emission systems to be sold in California, where state pollution standards are more stringent than elsewhere in the US and, possibly, anywhere else in the world.

This arrangement reflected the political conditions necessary to enact a federal air pollution control statute. It is a good case of politics in action. Because its unique geography and large population created severe air pollution problems, California wanted very strict limits on automobile emissions. Michigan, which is the home of the US automobile industry, wanted the law to be as lax as possible. For the whole country, they could agree on a middle position. But California would not go along unless it could set its own, more stringent standards, and California is a big state with enough votes to block a deal. So the statute said in effect: 'Fine, if you have a unique problem, you can do things differently.'[6]

In the intervening years, other states have adopted or have proposed adopting the California standards as well. In recent years, the major states on the East Coast from Boston to Washington D.C. have considered joint adoption of the California standards. This would mean that only certain kinds of automobiles could be sold and operated in those states. Were this to be done, you would have one set of pollution standards in two thirds of the country and a different set of standards in the remaining one third of the country.

This policy illustrates at least one form of flexibility that has been accepted in the United States. The regional approach has also been utilised in other policy

5 Two classic studies of this regulatory approach and its implications for federalism are A.W. Macmahon, *Administering Federalism in a Democracy*, New York, 1972; and D.R. Beam, et. al, *Regulatory Federalism: Policy, Process, Impact, and Reform*, Washington, U.S. Advisory Commission on Intergovernmental Relations, 1984.

6 An analysis of this case can be found in C.O. Jones, *Clean Air: The Policies and Politics of Pollution Control*, Pittsburgh, University of Pittsburgh Press, 1975.

areas, such as nuclear waste disposal, where federal law encourages states to form regional groups or compacts to deal collectively with the disposal of low level nuclear wastes.[7] It may be a form of flexible cooperation that is relevant to policy makers in the European context as well.

7 For information on nuclear waste disposal, see R.Kearney and J.J. Stucker, "Interstate Compacts and the Management of Low Level Radioactive Wastes," *Public Administration Review* 45, Jan-Feb 1985, p. 210-20; and B.Rabe, *Beyond Nimby: Hazardous Waste Siting in Canada and the United States*, Washington, 1994.

CHAPTER VII

Differentiation or Enhanced Cooperation

Formalizing Flexibility

Annemarie Lansdaal

1 Introduction

The coming accession of the countries of Central and Eastern Europe to the European Union will increase heterogeneity within the European Union and will further delay decision making. The risk of a less decisive Union formed, among other things, an occasion for the Intergovernmental Conference of 1996 and a review of the Maastricht Treaty. The result was the Treaty of Amsterdam. The so-called 'flexibility clauses' in the Treaty enable a majority of the fifteen Member States to proceed under strict conditions with an enhanced cooperation in a certain field and to use the Union's institutions. These clauses were created in order to release the tension between two different objectives: on the one hand deepening the integration and on the other hand enlargement to Central and Eastern European Countries. The Treaty of Nice relaxed the clauses for the same reasons. In short, flexibility has been formalised to prevent stagnation of European integration.

Institutionalisation of flexibility is a new issue in the history of European integration, but flexibility itself is not. Ever since the beginning of European integration there have been situations in which *other* forms of integration were chosen, in other words 'differentiation'. Differentiation deviates from 'traditional' integration where all Member States pursue simultaneously the same objectives.

Depending on the criteria laid down, there are many examples of differentiation and even more expressions in different languages. One could mention *e.g.* two speed, *plusieurs niveaux, Harter Kern,* pick-and-choose, *cercles excentriques, Abgestufte Integration, à la carte,* flying geese, multi-tier and *géométrie variable.* This motley collection of expressions gives rise to confusion.

The concept of 'flexibility' perhaps could become clearer when one looks at the gradual change in terminology on the basis of the most important forms of flexibility.

2 Multi-speed Europe

In the seventies, a diversity of ideas within the European Communities led to stagnation of European integration. In 1975, Leo Tindemans made a plan to give form to the European Union, and to introduce differentiation according to speed: a two tier Europe or a multi-tier Europe. Because of considerable financial and economic differences between the then nine Member States, it was no longer possible to integrate at the same speed. Tindemans feared his plans for a European Union would be unsuccessful due to the less developed members and due to the requirement of unanimity voting. He proposed a new approach that consisted on the one hand of accepting the *im*possibility of developing a plan whereby all Member States integrate simultaneously and on the other of creating an obligation to integrate further for those members that are capable of doing so, on conditions that further integration is based on a programme accepted by all Member States and that the common community context is guaranteed. Members that are not capable of proceeding have a right to assistance in order to catch up with the others as quickly as possible.

A multi-speed Europe thus indicates that all Member States pursue the same objective, whilst the realisation of this objective is done at different speeds. Tindemans underlines that he certainly was not in favour of an 'Europe *à la carte*' and that in the end all Member States must strive for the same level of integration. He also referred to Article 306 (ex Article 233 EC) of the EC Treaty that already permitted a temporary higher level of integration for the Benelux countries.

The immediate reaction to Tindemans' proposal was negative, but in the end one of the most important fields in European integration was harmonised according to a multi-speed principle: the Economic and Monetary Union.

3 Europe à la carte

Europe *à la carte* means that all Member States can choose their field of integration, without being bound to other fields. There is no longer a common objective, nor a common basis of at least some very important fields where all Member States travel the same path. Every member is free to compose the 'integration menu' of his choice. The Social Protocol, designed during the preparatory stage of the Maastricht Treaty as an answer to the British refusal to participate in a common social policy is the most important example of *à la carte* integration. It is differentiation in its most extreme form, for it leaves Member States total freedom in their choice to participate in a certain field of integration. Therefore, it is also a frightful image for those Member States that want to go on with European integration.

4 Variable geometry

This is a third important form of differentiated integration. This form brings difference in both the speed of integration and in the ultimate objective of integration. Thus integration is pursued in different fields, at a different speed and with different objectives. This so-called geographic version divides Europe into a 'core' and a 'periphery' of states surrounding the core. The core consists of the most developed members, the periphery encompasses those members that are not (yet) willing or able to keep up with the core. According to

Alexander Stubb, who under the supervision of William Wallace wrote a PhD on flexibility, the distinction between variable geometry and *à la carte* integration is as follows:

'The main distinction between variable geometry and à la carte *is that the former exemplifies a certain opt-in or opt-up to a conglomeration of Member States which have already pursued deeper integration in a specific policy area* (e.g. *the Schengen Agreements). The latter, on the other hand, is a form of differentiation in which a Member State opts out or opts down away from a specific policy area* (e.g. *the UK and the Social Chapter).'*[1]

This form of differentiation has as an important characteristic in that it takes place outside the European Union context and allows a permanent difference between Member States, in contradiction to multi-speed integration. Even though variable geometry sticks to a minimal common basis, it encompasses a greater risk that Europe will be divided into an elite (the advanced core) and those that lag behind. This may lead to a two class Europe, which should be prevented.

The three forms of differentiation given do not provide good alternatives for Europe. Europe *à la carte* will probably provoke further fragmentation instead of integration. Multi-speed Europe demands that all Member States are willing to reach the same objectives. The Social Protocol made it very clear that this demand is not always realistic, for not every Member State wants to go as far as the others in the integration of a certain field. Finally, variable geometry entailed the risk of dividing European citizens in two 'classes'.

Thus yet another way had to be found to reach more uniformity within the Union. Discussion over this new form of integration took from September 1994 to the end of the IGC of 1996. Numerous proposals and a diversity of expressions were passed in revue, until finally the terms 'flexibility' and 'enhanced cooperation' remained. The following paragraph gives a short description of the evolution of the terminology and the ideas of the different European actors, that eventually led to the institutionalisation of 'flexibility'.

5 On the eve of the 1996 IGC

At the European Council meeting at Corfu in June 1994, the decision was taken to create a discussion group assigned to prepare the agenda for the IGC of 1996. This 'Reflection Group', presided by Carlos Westendorp and

[1] A.C-G Stubb, " Categorization of Differentiated Integration", *Journal of Common Market Studies*, Vol. 34, No. 2 , 1996, p. 289.

composed of the personal representatives of the Ministries of Foreign Affairs, a representative of the European Commission and two representatives of the European Parliament, started its activities in June 1995 and reported on a possible review of the Maastricht Treaty at the end of 1995. Nevertheless the creation of the Reflection Group was not the starting point of the discussions on a new form of integration.

In September 1994, the German Christian-democrats CDU/CSU published a paper *'Überlegungen zur europäischen Politik'*. This paper is also known as the Lamers-Schäuble document, named after Karl Lamers, Foreign Affairs spokesman of the party and Wolfgang Schäuble, president of the working group that published it.

This document made several observations. Firstly that Europe was in a critical phase, and if a solution did not present itself within four years, Europe was going to become a collection of more or less independent states. The working group named as an important cause the size of the institutions of the Union, which was causing the Union to come apart at the seams. The institutions were created for six member states, and at the time the document was written they worked for twelve Member States and from 1995 for fifteen. The second observation concerned the growing number of members, which brought a divergence of interests and concerns and made it harder to agree on common objectives. These factors were influenced by other problems, such as a changing economic structure, unemployment and a growing nationalism. The working group also raised the question of when and how Central and Eastern European Countries should integrate into the European Union.

The CDU-CSU paper also elaborated five ideas. The first regards the development of the institutions of the Union and a more intensified application of the subsidiarity principle; more powers should be transposed to a lower level of decision making. The paper argues that no country should use its veto to frustrate members willing to integrate. It further states that it is necessary to develop a more flexible approach towards integration:

> *'En dépit de difficultés juridiques et pratiques considérables, l'idée de "géométrie variable" et d'une Europe "à plusieurs vitesses" devrait être autant que possible entérinée et institutionnalisée dans le Traité sur l'Union (...).Sinon, l'Union restera limitée à une coopération intergouvernementale favorable à "une Europe à la carte".'*[2]

In the second proposal, the working group aims to strengthen the Union's 'hard core'. This core should prevent Europe from fragmentation due to enlargement; the core integrates in all policy fields and should encourage further integration.

---

[2] *Europe/documents* No. 1895/96. Brussels, Agence internationale d'information pour la presse, 7-9-1994, p. 5-6.

Germany, France and the Benelux-countries are seen as the axis of Europe. Italy, number six at the creation of the European Communities in the fifties, is not part of the core as seen by the CDU/CSU working group. The 'hard core' of members should be accessible for other states, on the condition that they satisfy entrance criteria and are willing to participate.

The other three proposals insist on an intensification of Franco-German relations, on a strengthening of the Union's decisiveness in Common Foreign and Security Policy, and on enlargement towards the East. The plans given in the Lamers-Schäuble document are sometimes summarised as 'a multi-speed Europe surrounding a hard core'.

In a reaction to the German document, the then French Prime Minister Balladur gave an interview to the French newspaper *Le Figaro* on 30 August 1994. His vision of a future Europe consisted of three concentric circles. Balladur distinguished three systems within Europe. The first concerns an economic organisation that embraces all members of the European Union and, shortly put, the common market. This is more or less the basic system, that also functions as a common law system.

A second system consists of a small group of Member States that closely cooperate in monetary and military matters. This already happens within Franco-German relations, and would have to be expanded. Finally, all Member States will participate in this system.

A final system given by Balladur is Europe in total, *i.e.* with inclusion of the countries that for the time being will not be official members of European Union, but with whom diplomatic and economic relations should be established. It is the intention that these three concentric circles will come together and will finally merge into two circles or maybe even one. Balladur argues that Europe's largest task is diversification through enlargement while keeping an effective hard core.

Both the Lamers-Schäuble document and Balladur distinguish a hard core and a periphery, characteristic of a variable geometry. Balladur's version is more flexible than the German proposal, for Lamers and Schäuble state that there is a fixed sequence to come from periphery to hard core, the highest level of integration. This sequence is determined historically. Balladur does not put this condition, he gradually adapts his ideas in the course of November 1994 and changes 'concentric' circles into 'ex-centric' circles: a Europe of several groups and cores that overlap.

Most Member States reacted defensively to the plans, for they feared exclusion from the hard core and a place in the periphery, second-rate position. Also not everyone was grateful to Lamers and Schäuble for pointing out the hard core (Benelux, Germany and France). Yet this might have caused an uplift of the discussion and the active participation of (almost) all Member States.

The then British Prime Minister John Major explicitly mentioned the term 'flexibility' for the first time during a speech held at Leyden University on 7 September 1994. He opted for a multi-speed Europe and clearly rejected the idea of variable geometry. He thought that a hard core of Member States or even a hard core of policies entailed the risk that members are kept out instead of members being able to decide for themselves whether they join in or not. Major argued in favour of more flexibility, *i.e.* a greater freedom of choice. His version of flexibility sides with the *à la carte* form.

Chancellor Kohl's reaction is: *'Le bateau le plus lent du convoi ne peut dicter le rythme et le développement européen'.*[3] This position was the starting point for the idea of creating smaller cooperation units within European Union, where the members willing and able to integrate are no longer held up by those unwilling. In a letter dated December 1995, Helmut Kohl and Jacques Chirac for the first time officially mention 'enhanced cooperation' and its insertion in the Treaty.

The term flexibility is then found in the report of the Reflection Group of December 1995. The Reflection Group rejects Europe *à la carte*, but states that possibilities for flexibility should be examined, in order to give shape to diversity within the European Union without subordinating the *acquis communautaire* and the common objectives. In its formulation of six criteria, the Reflection Group draws the context within which flexible cooperation could take place. It sets as the most important criterion the conservation of a common basis.

The six criteria are: respect and preservation of the *acquis communautaire*; strengthening of the unique institutional context; authorisation of only temporary differences; no exclusion of members that meet the entrance conditions and want to join in; help for those who lag behind; use of flexibility clauses as a last resort and on a case by case basis. The fifth criterion, of help for the ones who stay behind was also present in the Tindemans report. This criterion disappears later on in the discussions.

The report of the Reflection Group put 'flexibility' definitely on the agenda of the IGC that started in March 1996 in Turin.

6 The 1996 Intergovernmental Conference

In September 1996 a blueprint for a new Treaty appeared. This was the first legal text. By then it was agreed that flexibility should find its way into the new Treaty, but its form was not yet clear. Different descriptions or definitions passed the revue.

---

[3] *Europe/Political Day* No. 6310. Brussels, agence internationale d'information pour la presse, 8-9-1994, p. 2.

Thus, a Franco-German proposal of October 1996 stated that such flexible cooperation has as its objective deepening of European integration, even if in the beginning only some of the Member States are prepared to integrate further. Such a provision should allow forms of enhanced cooperation that otherwise would take place outside the European Union to grow within a community context.

The Franco-German document proposed to formulate a number of fundamental principles that need to be respected in all three Union pillars, and next to those a number of separate provisions for each pillar. Procedures should be kept as simple as possible and competing circles avoided. Next to this, the *acquis* should be protected and the institutions should keep their actual tasks and powers.

The concept Treaty presented in Dublin at the end of the Irish presidency did not contain any detailed legal proposal, but it summed up the points of agreement and the problems in relation to flexibility:

'La question de ce qu'il est convenu d'appeler "flexibilité", la "coopération renforcée" ou encore "l'intégration différenciée", c'est-à-dire la possibilité pour un nombre d'États membres de coopérer plus étroitement dans certains domaines en utilisant le cadre institutionnel de l'Union, est l'une des questions les plus importantes qu'examine la Conférence. Ce qui sera décidé à cet égard – ou, a contrario, l'absence de décision – revêtira une importance extrême pour l'avenir de l'Union.'[4]

The unsolved points or problems mentioned by the Dublin concept are for a major part solved by an Italian concept text of January 1997. It forms an important contribution to the institutionalisation of flexibility, for the document is the basis for the Dutch concept provisions. Among other things, the form that the Franco-German document of October 1996 proposed is preserved; a common part with complementary provisions for each pillar.

7 The IGC 2000: return of variable geometry?

Closer cooperation, the official term used in the Amsterdam Treaty, was to be subject of reform in the Nice Treaty. The main instigator of the discussions was the French president Jacques Chirac. In an address to the German *Bundestag* on 27 June 2000, he evoked the possibility of forming a 'pioneer-group':

---

[4] Document CONT 2500/96 in SEC 48/4, p. 128.

'C'est aussi de l'approfondissement des politiques, à l'initiative de ces pays que j'évoquais tout à l'heure et qui souhaitent aller plus loin ou plus vite. Rassemblés avec l'Allemagne et la France, ils pourraient se constituer en un "groupe pionnier". Ce groupe ouvrirait la voie en s'appuyant sur la nouvelle procédure de coopération renforcée définie par la CIG et en nouant, si nécessaire, des coopérations hors traité, mais sans jamais remettre en cause la cohérence et l'acquis de l'Union.'[5]

The effect of his speech resembled the effect the Lamers-Schaüble document had in 1994. Though Chirac did not point out the members of the pioneer-group, he certainly suggested formation of a hard core surrounding the Franco-German tandem. It caused an uplift of the discussion on closer cooperation.

Chirac's proposal can be ranged under the heading of 'variable geometry'; it includes the risk of leading to two 'classes' of European Member States. Chirac tries to appease those who fear the formation of a hard core by adding that the group must remain open for those who want to join it. Nevertheless, the proposed secretariat that coordinates and watches over the coherence of the positions and policies of participating states does lead to think that Chirac envisages the creation of a permanent core-group. His brief remark about setting up, if necessary, cooperation outside the context of the Treaties only contributes to the alerting effect his speech has on the IGC of 2000.[6]

The Nice Treaty recognizes the need to relax the flexibility provisions. At the same time, it tries to give guarantees against the forming of a permanent 'hard core'.[7] Nice does thus not accept the 'variable geometry' concept proposed by Chirac.

The change of its formal name from 'closer cooperation' to 'enhanced cooperation' occurs in the English version of the Treaty. A short check with some other versions of the Treaty learns that the formal name also changes in the Danish version, but not in the French, German, Dutch, Italian or Spanish versions. As the IGC documents do not provide any information on the change of name, we must presume that the shift to 'enhanced cooperation' is only made to bring the English version more in line with the other language versions of the Nice Treaty.

---

5 *Notre Europe*, discours de M. Jacques Chirac Président de la République devant le Bundestag (Reichstag, Berlin, Allemagne – 27 June 2000), published in *Le Monde* of 28 June 2000, also available on http://www.elysee.fr/europe/discours/disc000627.htm.

6 See *e.g.* the Select Committee on Foreign Affairs *Sixth Report*, House of Commons' Report on the IGC, 11 July 2000.

7 See the contributions of respectively Annette Schrauwen (Chapter VIII) and Tom Eijsbouts (Chapter XII) to this volume.

8 Flexibility: differentiation and enhanced cooperation

The term flexibility is present from the beginning of the discussions on new forms of integration, but depending on who uses the term, its content changes over and over. In the course of the debates on the new form of integration that must prevent European fragmentation, flexibility gradually gets to signify differentiation – though at the start of the debates different forms are discussed (variable geometry, concentric circles, multi-speed, etcetera). Later on during the 1996 IGC, when flexibility is elaborated in detail, it presents more and more the figure of 'enhanced cooperation'. This figure is under attack in the 2000 IGC, but manages to survive in a slightly modified form.

In brief, flexibility has two meanings. One is a very general meaning, *i.e.* flexibility as a deviation from traditional integration. This can signify a differentiation in speed or integration-pace, as is present in Economic and Monetary Union, but also a differentiation in objective or field of integration. Here, flexibility equals differentiation.

The second meaning of flexibility specifically refers to the most recent form of differentiation: the flexibility clauses of the Amsterdam and Nice Treaties that allow enhanced cooperation within European Union institutional context.

CHAPTER VIII

Flexibility from Amsterdam to Nice

An Overview

dr. Annette Schrauwen

1 Introduction

The idea of flexibility – under the provocative name of 'hard core' – was launched in a CDU/CSU document written by Wolfgang Schäuble and Karl Lamers.[1] It reappeared in subsequent declarations and under different names[2] to end up under the term 'strengthened cooperation' in the formal mandate to the IGC, given by the Turin European Council of 29 March 1996:

'The heads of State or Government ask the Conference to examine whether and how to introduce rules either of a general nature or in specific areas in order to enable a certain number of Member States to develop a strengthened co-operation, open to all, compatible with the Union's objectives, while preserving the acquis communautaire, avoiding discrimination and distortions of competition and respecting the single institutional framework.'[3]

On 17 October 1996 an official Franco-German IGC proposal for 'enhanced cooperation' gave a number of conditions for its functioning: preservation of the single institutional context, preservation of the *acquis communautaire*, no veto by a single Member State, no possibility of Treaty modification within a context of flexible cooperation, no exclusion of any Member State willing and able to participate.[4]

The Amsterdam Treaty includes flexibility under the formal name of 'closer cooperation' in the first and third pillars. In the second pillar, the Treaty introduces a different form of flexibility, known as 'constructive abstention'. The Amsterdam Treaty repeats the given conditions, but in a different degree of strictness. Basically, one can make a hierarchy of 'strictness'.[5] Flexibility in the first pillar (EC) has to fulfil the most strict conditions. In the second pillar (Common Foreign and Security Policy), flexibility is the least hindered by enabling conditions, whilst the remaining third pillar (Police and Judicial Cooperation in Criminal Matters) is to be found in the middle.

---

1 Wolfgang Schäuble and Karl Lamers, Reflections on European policy, 1 september 1994.

2 See the contribution of A. Lansdaal to the present volume, Chapter VII.

3 Presidency Conclusions, Turin European Council, 29 March 1996, Nr. SN100/1/96, pt. 2

4 Franco-german proposal for Flexibility, CONF/3955/96.

5 See A.C-G. Stubb, "Negotiating Flexible Integration in the Amsterdam Treaty", in K. Neunreither and A. Wiener, *European Integration After Amsterdam. Institutional Dynamics and Prospects for Democracy*, Oxford, 2000, p. 153-174. The initial version of my contribution found inspiration in the speech Alexander Stubb made on the conference *Flexibility in Federal Constitutions*, held in Amsterdam on 15 May 1998.

Though not all Member States agreed on the need for reform of the provisions – why change 'procedures that were agreed only in 1997 and which have not yet been put to the test, or indeed used at all'[6] – it was felt that closer cooperation should be transformed into a more workable mechanism in order to face a growing diversity.[7] Halfway the IGC leading to the Nice Treaty, the Feira European Council in June 2000 decided that

'the provisions on closer co-operation introduced into the Treaty of Amsterdam should also form part of the IGC's work, while respecting the need for coherence and solidarity in an enlarged Union'.[8]

The Treaty of Nice, signed on 26 February 2001, changes the conditions for flexibility in the respective pillars of the EU Treaty. The introduction of proper flexibility provisions in the second pillar catches the eye. Other modifications concern a loosening of the criteria allowing closer cooperation in the first and third pillars. This contribution gives an overview of the flexibility provisions in the different pillars. It follows the road from Amsterdam to Nice and along the way distinguishes forms of flexibility according to the strictness of conditions.

2 General flexibility in the first and third pillars: a workable mechanism?

The Treaty of Amsterdam sets the framework for the general forms of flexibility in its Articles 43, 44 and 45 EU. They give the general criteria for closer cooperation, which mainly comes down to staying within the objectives and the institutional framework of the respective Treaties. Furthermore, closer cooperation should concern at least a majority of Member States and it should be open to all Member States at any time, provided they accept the concerned closer cooperation in full.

Both the EC Treaty as well as the Treaty on European Union carry provisions laying down additional criteria for closer cooperation. Article 11 EC[9] excludes

---

6 *IGC: Reform for Enlargement, The British Approach to the European Union Intergovernmental Conference 2000*, February 2000, CM 43595, point 76.

7 For an assessment of the need to change the Amsterdam closer cooperation provisions, see E. Philippart and Monika Sie Dhian Ho, *The Pros and Cons of 'Closer Co-operation' within the EU. Argumentation and Recommandations*, March 2000, WRR Working Document W104. Their main conclusion is that 'the interest of the Union is to revise the mechanism for closer co-operation as soon as possible', p. 43.

8 Presidency Conclusions, Santa Maria da Feira European Council, 19 and 20 june 2000, nr. 200/1/00, pt. 3.

9 See the contribution of E. Steyger to this volume, Chapter X.

from closer cooperation the areas which fall within the exclusive competence of the Community and matters concerning the citizenship of the Union. However, closer cooperation can only take place on the basis of existing Community competencies.

The additional third pillar criteria which Article 40 EU gives, do not exclude any field from closer cooperation but they demand respect for EC powers and third pillar objectives. The development of an area of freedom, security and justice is explicitly mentioned as one of the aims of closer cooperation.

The additional criteria both provisions give on authorization for closer cooperation and on members willing to participate in a later stage are very much identical. Authorization to start a form of closer cooperation is given by the Council in qualified majority voting; the Commission 'proposes' in first pillar flexibility and 'presents its opinion' in third pillar flexibility. There is however a veto mechanism, an 'emergency-brake' for Member States reluctant to let the others go ahead. In such a case, the Council may, by qualified majority, refer the matter to the European Council which will decide upon the matter unanimously. The formula that the reluctant Member State can thus block the closer cooperation 'for important and stated reasons of national policy' certainly brings to mind the Luxembourg Agreement of 1966. The emergency-brake was one of the main subjects under discussion in the Nice negotiations.

When Member States want to join in on cooperation already set up, they have to notify their intention to Council and Commission. In first pillar closer cooperation, the Commission decides on participation and possible specific arrangements, in third pillar closer cooperation the Council is the decision-making body. Third pillar provisions further permit the Council to hold the decision in abeyance and set a deadline for re-examining it.

The general flexibility provisions as formulated in the Amsterdam Treaty, also called the 'enabling clauses' were never put into practice. It has been argued that the Amsterdam conditions for achieving closer cooperation are 'so strict that they could never be used in practice'.[10] The first few months of 2000 show a growing interest in flexibility. Both European Commission and a number of member states argue in their IGC opinions that flexibility should be on the agenda.[11] The Portuguese presidency puts it on the agenda in June 2000.

At an early point in the discussions within the Group of Representatives and the Ministerial Conclave, the French presidency proposed to include a list of 'all of the (general and specific) conditions governing the triggering of closer

---

10 House of Lords, Select Committee on European Union, Eleventh Report, point 69.

11 Commission opinion, *Adapting the Institutions to make a success of enlargement*, COM (2000) 34, p. 33; Germany, the Netherlands, Belgium, Finland, Italy and Luxembourg wanted flexibility on the agenda of the IGC, see A. Stubb, "Dealing with flexibility in the IGC" in E. Best a.o. (eds.), *Rethinking the European Union. IGC 2000 and Beyond*, Maastricht, 2000, p. 145-157, p. 152.

cooperation' at the beginning of the Treaty text on closer cooperation.[12] It was believed to promote simplicity and clarity. Thus, the EC Treaty as amended by the Treaty of Nice will no longer set out additional criteria for closer cooperation in first or third pillar matters, but all enabling clauses are given together in the amended Article 43 EU. This result puts aside an idea that also came up during reform discussions, *e.g.* to make closer cooperation in areas at the heart of the integration process subject to more stringent requirements, so there would be different 'forms' of closer cooperation.[13] The amended Articles 11 EC and 40 EU set out each pillar's triggering procedure for closer cooperation, or 'enhanced cooperation' as it is called since Nice.[14] The amendments in both the general conditions of Article 43 EU and the respective triggering procedures in the first and third pillar are meant to make closer cooperation a more workable device.

The main changes to relax the triggering mechanisms concern the 'emergency-brake' and the role of the European Commission and the European Parliament. In brief, the emergency-brake does not recall the Luxembourg Agreement any more, though a member of the Council still may request that a decision on starting enhanced cooperation is put before the European Council. The relevant provisions no longer contain a reference to unanimity voting nor to 'important and stated reasons of national policy'. Commission and Parliament become more involved in the triggering procedure.[15]

The list of conditions for general closer cooperation was subject to several changes during the discussions. Some conditions were deleted, others were transferred and still others were added. The most important modification to make closer cooperation more workable seems to be the one that sets the minimum number of participants at eight Member States instead of at the majority of Member States.

Article 43 EU does not include all conditions that were previously spread out over Articles 11 EC and 43 EU. Firstly, European citizenship is no longer a forbidden subject for closer cooperation. On proposal from Italy and Germany the restriction on citizenship was removed, so that a limited number of Member states may for instance accord to European citizens on a closer cooperation basis the right to vote in country-wide elections.[16] The general restriction that closer cooperation must aim at further integration (Article 43(a) EU) presents a safeguard against any drawbacks in the development of European citizenship. The removal of the restrictions on citizenship was not without any discussion

---

[12] Presidency Note, 30 August 2000, CONFER 4766/00, p. 2.

[13] Presidency Note, 18 July 2000, CONFER 4761/00, pt 2.4.

[14] See the contribution of A. Lansdaal to the present volume, Chapter VII.

[15] See also the contribution of F. Goudappel, "The Influence of Flexibility on the Institutional Balance of the European Community and the European Union" to the present volume, Chapter IX.

[16] *Position paper from Germany and Italy*, CONFER 4783/00, 4 October 2000, p. 6.

though; during negotiations, the presidency came with a proposal in which citizenship was still excluded from closer cooperation.[17]

Secondly, the interests of non-participants are no longer explicitly protected in the Nice version of Article 43 EU, though closer cooperation still is to respect 'the competences, rights and obligations of those Member States who do not participate therein' (Article 43(h) EU). The word 'interests' implies political discretion and therefore the risk that closer cooperation will be obstructed by an unwilling Member State, as argued by Germany and Italy in their proposal to delete this word.[18] The same argument supports their proposal to delete Amsterdam's condition that flexibility is only used as a last resort, but that proposal didn't make it. Article 43a EU (Nice version) still includes the 'last resort' restriction and even adds an element of reason to it. The Council must establish that the relevant procedures of the Treaties cannot be applied to attain the objectives of such cooperation within a 'reasonable period'. Furthermore, the last resort clause in its Nice version says attainment of 'the objectives of such cooperation', where the Amsterdam version refers to attainment of 'the objectives of the said Treaties'. It is very likely that this modification does not bring any new element to the last resort clause[19], as Nice also added reinforcement of the process of integration as one of the aims of enhanced cooperation in Article 43 under (a).

Other conditions given in Amsterdam's Articles 11 EC and 43 EU were also subject to (subtle) modification. The proposed cooperation in the Nice version must respect 'the said Treaties' instead of the 'principles of the said Treaties', and it must 'respect' the *acquis communautaire* instead of 'not affect' it. As noted before, the most important modification can be found in the minimum number of participants. Amsterdam sets this minimum at the majority of Member States, Nice gives the number of at least eight Member States. This condition thus gets more flexible as the Union gets larger. The minimum of participants was subject to several changes in the succeeding proposal, but in the end it was set at eight. This number can be found in the proposals by Germany and Italy as well as in the Benelux memorandum with regard to the Intergovernmental Conference.[20]

---

17 *Note from the presidency*, CONFER 4780/00, 5 October 2000, p. 2. A few weeks later, a new note from the presidency does no longer consider citizenship as forbidden area for closer cooperation, CONFER 4786/00, 23 October 2000, p. 2.

18 *Position paper from Germany and Italy*, CONFER 4783/00, 4 October 2000, p. 4.

19 In his excellent analysis of the Nice closer cooperation provisions, F. Tuytschaever points at the possibility that the last resort clause makes closer cooperation independent from previously rejected proposals in the Council. See F. Tuytschaever, "Nauwere samenwerking volgens het Verdrag van Nice", *SEW*, November 2001, p. 375-387, pt. 45.

20 See respectively CONFER 4783/00, p. 4 and CONFER 4787/00, p.5.

A new condition to start enhanced cooperation can be found in Nice's modified Article 43(e) EU. Closer cooperation may not undermine the internal market nor the economic or social cohesion. The phrase seems to be inserted in a rather late stage of the negotiations, it can be first found in the proposals from the presidency of 9 November 2000.[21] Respect for economic and social cohesion is a safeguard condition against the risk formulated by the European Parliament that enhanced cooperation is used to create a 'hard core' of 'Member States which would, by reason of its cohesion and collective weight, end up directing the rest'.[22]

The risk of the 'hard core' idea is also tackled by giving the explicit mention that closer cooperation should be open to all Member States its own Article in Nice (Article 43b EU). Furthermore, this Article adds that the 'Commission and the Member States participating in enhanced cooperation shall ensure that as many Member States as possible are encouraged to take part'. To avoid the risk of a lack of cohesion, the Treaty provisions demand from the Council and the Commission to ensure the consistency of closer cooperation activities with the policies of the Union and the Community (Article 45 EU).

Nice mentions explicitly that acts and decisions for the implementation of closer cooperation shall not form part of the *Union acquis*. During negotiations, the presidency proposed to add a provision to Article 249 EC that would restrict their binding character to only the participating Member States.[23] Somehow, it got replaced by the remark in the last sentence of Article 44 par. 1 EU that implementation of closer cooperation is not part of the *acquis* of the Union. The word 'Union' suggests that the negotiators had in mind closer cooperation in the second and third pillar, but first pillar closer cooperation also falls under this provision according to Article 11 EC. Candidate members might find comfort in the fact that they will not be forced to live up to the aims of these closer cooperation forms, contrary to the predetermined[24] forms of flexibility such as EMU and the Area of freedom, security and justice.[25]

In conclusion, it might be said that all modifications express the wish to form a balance between the need to transform flexibility into a workable device and the risk of misuse of flexibility, *e.g.* to create either an *'à la carte Europe'* where there is no cohesion or a 'directorate' of Member States which would exclude the others from the decision-making centre and split Europe into two groups.

---

[21] CONFER 4798/00, p. 2.

[22] *Report on reinforced co-operation*, A-5-0288/2000(INI), rapporteur: José María Gil-Robles Gil Delgado, p. 10.

[23] CONFER 4803/00, 17 November 2000, p. 7.

[24] This is the term the Portuguese Presidency uses.

[25] See also F. Tuytschaever "Nauwere samenwerking volgens het Verdrag van Nice", *SEW*, November 2001, p. 375-387, pts. 40 and 44.

3 Introduction of flexibility in the second pillar

Amsterdam's second pillar's flexibility is a diluted form of flexibility. It is a clause which enables the Union to come to a decision in a particular situation, and which has nothing to do with the idea of 'enhanced cooperation'. Article 23, par. 1 EU stipulates that unanimous decisions will not be blocked by abstaining Member States, if the latter formally declare to abstain and to accept that the decision commits the Union. Only in the case of the abstaining members representing more than one third of the votes weighted for qualified majority[26], is the decision blocked. The 'constructive abstention' clause as it is called generally, contains no possibility for abstaining members to later on join the ones that took the initial decision. Mutual obligations are restricted to respect of the other party's decision (not) to participate and to act accordingly. Thus, this form of flexibility seems contrary to the original idea that flexible cooperation should have a temporary character and be open to all Member States. Can this be attributed to the fact that CFSP substantially differs from other fields of cooperation?

The main difficulty in taking CFSP-related decisions is lack of predictability.[27] The CFSP system is not a closed one as is the process of economic integration where all participating states are known. When deciding upon a common action in the field of CFSP, Member States never know beforehand what external parties are going to be involved or what the consequences (in terms of loss of international status, loss of financial means or even loss of human lives) will be. Substantive decisions will mostly be ad hoc, as they will not be anchored in internal legislation. Nor is there a competent tribunal to go to for appeal. All these elements turn second pillar decision-making into a tricky business; it is no wonder Member States are very reluctant in this field.

Reluctance in CFSP matters explains why Member States want to stick to unanimous decision-making. The diluted form of flexibility makes it possible for dissenting Member States not to bind themselves to a decision without blocking it. Where qualified majority voting is introduced in the second pillar, 'Mr. Blair's new formulation of the Luxembourg compromise'[28] still guarantees the members that they cannot be bound against their will: a vote shall not be taken when a member of the Council intends to oppose a decision 'for important and stated reasons of national policy'.[29]

---

[26] Art. 205(2) EC (ex Art. 148 EC).

[27] This observation draws on I. Davidson, "Gezamenlijk buitenlands beleid van Europa blijft een illusie", *NRC Handelsblad*, 4 November 1998, p. 9.

[28] See A. Duff, *The Treaty of Amsterdam. Text and Commentary*, London, 1997, p. 196.

[29] Art. 23, par. 2 EU (ex Art. J.13, par. 2).

Amsterdam's 'constructive abstention' clause is absolutely no guarantee that second pillar cooperation will progress.[30] It was expected however that the clause would help to overcome obstruction by reluctant members in unanimity decisions, even if on a case-by-case basis. The ad hoc character of CFSP makes it improbable that in a later stage abstaining members will want to participate in a decision. Nevertheless, in the negotiations leading up to Nice the second pillar got its own 'true' form of flexibility. In the early days of negotiations on flexibility, Spain came with a commented proposal to insert flexibility in the second pillar.[31]

Spain has made the point that constructive abstention is different from closer cooperation in that it 'implies an opposing position on the part of whoever exercises it', whereas closer cooperation does not necessarily imply a negative reaction from the ones unwilling or unable to participate.[32] Spain seems mostly concerned to bring European defence initiatives – such as the Euro-Corps – under the umbrella of the European Union. Here the analogy with Schengen is remarkable: closer cooperation permits the able and willing to go ahead within the Union structure. In this regard Spain diverges from the Belgian delegation, that considers closer cooperation not suited for defining policy, because the credibility and unity of the CFSP would be harmed if not all members participated. This concern led to the restriction of second pillar closer cooperation to implementation of a joint action or a common position only (Article 27b EU). Initial proposals to put in a protocol annexed to the Treaty a 'pre-defined closer cooperation' in the field of security and defence did not make it.[33]

Spain – later on supported by the position paper of Germany and Italy[34] – considers closer cooperation in particular suited for security and defence and the carrying out of the 'Petersberg missions'.[35] Remarkably the Nice Treaty excludes matters having military or defence implications from closer cooperation in its Article 27b EU. A few weeks before the Nice summit, the presidency's proposals on enhanced cooperation still included a specific provision in the field of security and defence.[36] The presidency recognised in the same document however, that delegations are divided on this issue. The exclusion of military

---

30 See for instance S. Nuttal, "L'Union Fait la Force: The ins and outs of the European's Foreign and Defence Policy," in *European Foreign Affairs Review*, 2000, p. 581-593.

31 CONFER 4760/00, 14 July 2000.

32 Idem, p. 3.

33 CONFER 4766/00, p. 5.

34 CONFER 4783/00, p. 2.

35 CONFER 4760/00, p. 4. The Petersberg missions are: humanitarian and rescue tasks, peace-keeping tasks and crisis management. These missions can be found in Article 17 par. 2 EU.

36 CONFER 4803/00, 17 November 2000, p. 8.

and defence matters can be seen as a victory for the UK, flanked by Sweden and Ireland.[37]

Nice introduces enhanced cooperation – next to the 'constructive abstention' – in the second pillar in Articles 27a-27e EU. These provisions show some differences with the general flexibility provisions of the first and third pillars, though Articles 43 to 45 EU (all general conditions and restrictions, last resort and open participation clauses as well as clauses on finance and consistency) also apply to second pillar closer cooperation. Enhanced cooperation in the second pillar also requires a minimum of eight Member States, though the initial proposals gave a minimum of three or five Member States.[38]

Second Pillar closer cooperation differs from the other pillars in its triggering procedure and the monitoring of its consistency. The triggering procedure in CFSP closer cooperation still has the throwback to the Luxembourg Compromise, which means that a single Member State can block closer cooperation for 'important and stated reasons of national policy' (Article 23 par. 2 EU). Second pillar matters are sensitive material for Member States. Monitoring consistency is also different in pillar two because of the involvement of the High Representative, who has his special responsibilities in implementing CFSP. Article 27d EU instructs him to fully inform the European Parliament and all members of the Council.

Second pillar flexibility is the Amsterdam version of flexibility. At the time of the signing of the Amsterdam Treaty, comments were that flexibility was not suited for CFSP, because it presupposed policy areas and not individual actions.[39] The only exception would be security and defence. Nice certainly defies the comments.

4 Flexibility in the area of freedom, security and justice: predetermined flexibility

The transfer of asylum and immigration matters from the third pillar to the first, and the integration of the Schengen *acquis* into the framework of the European Union, are as such forms of flexible cooperation. These were not modified in Nice.

---

[37] E. Best, "The Treaty of Nice: Not Beautiful but It'll Do", *Eipascope 2001/1*, p. 2-9, at p. 7; see also F. Tuytschaever "Nauwere samenwerking volgens het Verdrag van Nice", *SEW*, November 2001, p. 375-387, p. 379.

[38] See CONFER 4780/00, p. 4; CONFER 4783/00, p. 7; CONFER 4786/00, p. 6; CONFER 4803/00, p. 9.

[39] See S. Nuttal, "L'Union Fait la Force: The ins and outs of the European's Foreign and Defence Policy," in *European Foreign Affairs Review*, 2000, p. 581-593, p. 583.

4.1 Transfer of asylum and immigration matters

Neither the United Kingdom nor Ireland will participate in issues relating to free movement of persons, immigration and asylum. Denmark succeeded in keeping its opt-out from citizenship issues, which was encapsulated in a decision of the Heads of State or Government meeting within the European Council at Edinburgh in December 1992.[40] So neither will Denmark participate in decisions on free movement, immigration and asylum. Yet the two exceptions making asylum and immigration matters a form of flexible cooperation, United Kingdom and Ireland on the one hand, Denmark on the other, do not have the same limitations and restrictions.

The United Kingdom and Ireland were very keen to ensure that their border controls remain intact. Ireland seems more willing to participate in the common policies of the Union, but is withheld by 'its wish to maintain its common travel area with the United Kingdom in order to maximise freedom of movement into and out of Ireland.'[41] In the event that Ireland chooses to take part in issues relating to free movement, immigration and asylum, it only has to notify the President of the Council in writing and the normal Treaty provisions will apply to it (Protocol, Article 8). The United Kingdom and Ireland may also take part in the debate about and decisions on free movement, immigration and asylum decisions on an ad hoc basis. But if no decision can be reached with the participation of the United Kingdom and Ireland, they may be by-passed by the other Member States, who may adopt a decision which will not bind the United Kingdom or Ireland. After decisions have been made, the United Kingdom or Ireland may notify the Commission that it wants to participate. Then the 'general' flexibility clause of Article 11(3) – after Nice Article 11a – of the EC Treaty will apply (Protocol, Article 4).

Denmark will not participate in decisions relating to free movement, apart from decisions concerning visas based on former first pillar competence, old Article 100C EC. Denmark cannot opt-in on the decision-making process, but it can decide to accept a completed directive. The obligation will then be under international law, not under European Community law.

4.2 Integration of Schengen

The Protocol integrating Schengen into the Union framework (Protocol No. 2) concerns not only the abstaining members United Kingdom, Ireland and Denmark, but also the associated members Iceland and Norway who

[40] OJ no. C 348, 31.12.92, p.1.

[41] See Declaration by Ireland on Article 3 of the Protocol on the Position of the United Kingdom and Ireland.

are not Member States of the Union. Of the abstaining members there is only one, Denmark, who actually is a party to the Schengen Agreements but not participating in the integration of the *acquis* into the Union. The development of the Schengen *acquis* is going to be a very complex issue, where decisions can be adopted by either twelve, fourteen or sixteen members, but never fifteen.

The Council, consisting of the thirteen Member States that are both Schengen and EU members, shall unanimously determine the legal basis (first pillar or third pillar provisions) for each act of the Schengen *acquis*. Thus, Denmark will participate in decisions on the legal basis of Schengen issues. However, Denmark is not bound by Schengen acts based on first pillar provisions, but remains party to the Schengen Agreement. Whenever the Council decides to build upon the Schengen *acquis* under the first pillar, Denmark may decide to implement this decision in its internal law and it will create an obligation under international law between Denmark and the other twelve EU-Schengen members. If the Council has not reached a decision on legal bases for the Schengen *acquis*, the acts will be regarded as based upon third pillar provisions from the date of entry into force of the Amsterdam Treaty and its Protocols. There is no such thing as predetermined flexibility in third pillar issues; Denmark has no opt-out as in the first pillar.

The opt-out of the United Kingdom and Ireland from the Schengen integration is only a bit more consistent with the 'general' form of flexibility applying to the first and third pillars. The two non-members of Schengen remain outside the *acquis*, unless they request to join in part or all of the *acquis*. In that case, the Council decides unanimously on the request. In the event the United Kingdom or Ireland want to participate in measures that build upon the integrated *acquis*, they can do so according to the methods provided for issues related to free movement, immigration and asylum (see above). However, new EU members will have to accept the Schengen *acquis* and all measures built upon it in full. This is a surprising provision in a context where the possibility of ad hoc opt-ins for Union members exists.

Norway and Iceland, members of Schengen, shall be associated with the implementation of the Schengen *acquis*. To that end, an Agreement will be signed with them. Thus, the Schengen *acquis* integrated in the first pillar has the status of international law for Denmark and the status of EC law for the others (including the United Kingdom and Ireland in domains where they opt in to the Schengen *acquis*).

The predetermined form of flexibility relating to free movement of persons is very flexible indeed, it is a complex of op-outs and *à la carte* integration. It differs from the general flexibility clauses in the way it deals with those who want to stay out: United Kingdom, Ireland and Denmark. Instead of general conditions on joining in on the area of free movement, each of these countries got their own conditions on participating in certain decisions. The respective declarations and protocols show a differentiation in involvement of those three members. Ireland is involved, but seems trapped by its passport union with the UK. The Danes for their part keep Schengen outside the Community system altogether.

The predetermined flexibility in the Area of Freedom, Security and Justice is an '*à la carte*' flexibility for the UK and Ireland. The provisions in relation to Denmark are not typically '*à la carte*'. Denmark chose the children's menu, because the Community context for free movement of persons was too much.

5 In conclusion: convenient flexibility

It seems that roughly four types of concerns have brought the concept of flexibility on the agenda.[42] Together they set the possibilities as well as the limits to the flexibility provisions:

a) A growing awareness that the IGC is no longer the main instrument for enhancing integration: the pace would be determined by the unable and/or unwilling member states.
b) The imminent enlargement of the Union will bring with it a greater heterogeneity of interests, which cannot be bridged by transition periods, at least not in a credible manner.
c) The 'core' Member States should get the possibility to realize their ambitions within the EU-context, without being frustrated by the unable/ unwilling. Flexibility becomes an instrument to bind the potentiality and ambition of 'leading' Member States to the Union.
d) As an *a contrario* argument, flexibility is a weapon against weakening and stagnation of the Union.

The main context however, was to realise all this without the risk that the Union would be divided into an elite 'hard core' and those lagging behind.[43]

Flexibility in CFSP comes in two forms: the diluted form of 'constructive abstention' and the more solid form of 'enhanced cooperation'. Both forms have in common the implicit guarantee for unwilling members that they are always able to block a 'flexible' decision by voting against it in the European Council. This is entirely compatible with the ad hoc character of CFSP, as described above. However both forms have their flaws as shown by Nuttal. The 'constructive abstention' clause might harm the credibility of CFSP in that it is difficult for the outside world to understand that any member can abstain itself from

---

[42] See J. Janning, "Differenzierung als Integrationsprinzip: die Flexibilität im neuen EU-Vertrag", in W. Weidenfeld (ed.), *Amsterdam in der Analyse. Strategien für Europa*, Gütersloh, 1998, p. 203-217.

[43] See the contribution of Annemarie Lansdaal to this volume, Chapter VII.

an ad hoc decision. The 'enhanced cooperation clauses' are not very suitable for CFSP matters, for the subjects are so interconnected in this area.[44]

Flexibility provisions in matters of free movement and asylum are a substantive elaboration of the wish of willing members to go on. Here, flexible cooperation clearly binds the ambitions of the 'leading' Member States to the Union. They are no longer forced to cooperate outside Union context, as was the case with Schengen.

The 'general' flexibility provisions, the enabling clauses, are the ones that in Amsterdam were most strict in limiting possible fields of cooperation. This has been qualified as 'inflexible flexibility' or 'Placebo' for Franco-German cooperation.[45] It seems that the reluctant members managed to stick to their reluctance regarding future particular forms of flexible cooperation. In Nice the unwilling had to give way in some respects. Their major loss probably is the veto-right in the first and third pillars, now that Article 40a EU no longer explicitly mentions unanimity voting in the European Council. Neither does the Nice text restrict referral to the European Council 'for important and stated reasons of national policy.' But referral to the European Council is still possible, by any Member of the Council. After the European Council has discussed the issue, the Council can grant authorisation by qualified majority.

However, the reluctant may have lost their veto but they were not defeated in Nice. As enhanced cooperation must remain open to all member states, the unwilling can – in Tuytschaever's words – apply the motto 'if you can't beat them, join them'.[46]

The stakes at Nice were to turn flexibility into a workable device. Fixing the minimum of participants to a closer cooperation at eight is the only modification made in Nice that clearly relaxes the enhanced cooperation option. The relaxation will especially be effective after the enlargement of the European Union.

The Nice provisions still carry the signs of a two-fold objective: link the ambitions of the willing to the EU context and prevent them from forming an avant-garde. It will be very interesting to see whether the flexibility provisions are flexible enough to keep the willing within the EU structure.

---

[44] S. Nuttal, "L'Union Fait la Force: The ins and outs of the European's Foreign and Defence Policy," in *European Foreign Affairs Review*, 2000, p. 581-593, p. 583.

[45] See J. Janning, "Differenzierung als Integrationsprinzip: die Flexibilität im neuen EU-Vertrag", in W. Weidenfeld (ed.), *Amsterdam in der Analyse. Strategien für Europa*, Gütersloh, 1998, p. 203-217, p. 215.

[46] F. Tuytschaever "Nauwere samenwerking volgens het Verdrag van Nice", *SEW*, November 2001, p. 375-387, p. 384, pt. 39; see also the contribution of Tom Eijsbouts to the present volume, Chapter XII.

CHAPTER IX

The Influence of Flexibility on the Institutional Balance of the European Community and the European Union

dr. Flora Goudappel

1 Introductory remarks

1.1 Introduction

What the notion of 'subsidiarity' was for the Treaty of Maastricht, 'flexibility' or 'closer cooperation' as it was officially labelled in the Treaty of Amsterdam, appears to be for the Treaty of Amsterdam: a new notion, the application of which is not clear yet, especially since it was re-labelled 'enhanced cooperation' in the Treaty of Nice. However, the confusion for subsidiarity concerned the relations between the European Union – and in particular the European Community – and the Member States, whereas the confusion surrounding flexibility is caused by the cases of applicability on one side and the position of the European institutions on the other.

In this study, the emphasis will be laid on the position of the European institutions when functioning under the system of flexibility and the accompanying legislative process. It will be approached from a constitutional point of view. By 'European institutions' in this context, there will mainly be reference to the Commission, the Council of Ministers, and the European Parliament. Although very important, the Court of Justice plays a different part because it is not one of the legislative bodies. Because of an emphasis on the legislative elements, the Court of Justice has to stay outside the scope of this study.

In advance, the question needs to be answered what the position of these European institutions is at the moment. Does an institutional balance exist at present? The answer to this question depends on the view on what an institutional balance is. It concerns a problem which is usually connected to the position of the European Parliament opposite the Council of Ministers and the Commission. Case law[1] and literature[2] start from the assumption that there exists a kind of institutional balance, a system of checks and balances. However, this does not necessarily mean that it is an ideal balance showing equality in position for the institutions. Each new treaty constitutes its own new institutional balance. Simultaneously, it is often said that the powers of the European Parliament are not sufficient for it to be considered a parliament in the true sense of the word. More powers and more efficient powers are therefore needed for the European Parliament in order to install an ideal institutional balance and to diminish the democratic deficit.[3]

Closely connected to the problem of an institutional balance, is the possible process towards federalization of the European Union, which is expected by

---

1 For instance Case C-70/88, *Parliament v. Council (Tsjernobyl)*[1990] ECR I-2041, pt. 27.

2 Kapteyn-VerLoren van Themaat, *Inleiding tot het recht van de Europese Gemeenschappen, Na Maastricht*, Deventer, 1995, p. 34.

3 *Ibid*, p. 270-271.

some[4] and feared by others.[5] After all, some European institutions reflect more the interests of the Member States, and others more the interests of the European Union.[6] Thus, the institutional balance indirectly implies a balance between European Union and Member States.

1.2 The procedures

When one considers the notion of flexibility as introduced in the Treaty of Amsterdam, in view of the institutional balance, the following description can be given. Flexibility is flexibility for a limited number – but still a majority[7] – of Member States to come to a form of enhanced cooperation in a specific policy field; closer than the cooperation there now is under the Treaties. The opting-out for the social paragraph by the United Kingdom, the Social Protocol and the EMU system were forerunners of this system. It was generally referred to by the use of terms such as 'Europe *à la carte*' or 'Europe of different speeds'.[8] In general, it can be said that flexibility has been introduced directly into the first and the third pillar of the European Union. For the second pillar, it was decided against the inclusion of flexibility,[9] although there are still possibilities for closer cooperation in this pillar[10], which fall outside the scope of this study. The Treaty of Nice elaborates the flexibility provisions of the Amsterdam Treaty and introduces flexibility in the second pillar.

The Amsterdam Treaty introduced three new main procedures in the European system: one in the first pillar and one in the third pillar, as well as the general procedure for flexibility which has been laid down in the EU Treaty. The competencies of the institutions differ in each of these procedures, which are mostly based on the previously existing procedures in the first pillar.

The general procedure for both the first and the third pillar, has been laid down in Articles 43-46 EU, which together form the 'Provisions on enhanced cooperation'. Comparing the provisions on closer cooperation in the Treaty of Amsterdam with the provisions on enhanced cooperation in the Treaty of Nice,

---

4 For instance: R.R. Bowie, "The Process of Federating Europe", in: A.W. Macmahon (ed.), *Federalism, Mature and Emergent*, New York, 1962, p. 493-509; or J. Kühnhardt, *Europäische Union und föderale Idee. Europapolitik in der Umbruchzeit*, Münich, 1993.

5 F.A.N.J. Goudappel, *Powers and Control Mechanisms in European Federal Systems*, Deventer, 1997, p. 2-3.

6 *Ibid*, p. 211-226.

7 Art. 43 sub d EU.

8 R. Barents, *Het Verdrag van Amsterdam*, Deventer, 1997, p. 30.

9 J.W. de Zwaan, "Het Verdrag van Amsterdam, een overzicht", *Nederlands Tijdschrift voor Europees Recht*, February 1998, p. 38.

10 By means of Art. 23 sub 1 EU. See also C.D. Ehlermann, "Les nouvelles dispositions du traité d'Amsterdam", *Revue du Marché Unique Européen* 3/1997, p. 81-82.

there is an apparent shift in approach to the possibility of flexibility. In the Treaty of Amsterdam, general provisions were laid down concerning closer cooperation while listing the possibilities. From Nice onwards, flexibility will only be used as a last resort and later entry by non-participating Member States is always open. The position of the European Parliament has been strengthened; flexibility is not anymore limited to the initiatives of the Council as such. Much power is shared by Council and Commission.

In the first pillar, the procedure concerning enhanced cooperation has been laid down in Articles 11 and 11a EC. Article 11 concerns the procedure itself; Article 11a EC concerns the procedure for Member States wishing to participate later on. The basic procedure consists of the Member States asking the Commission for authorization for enhanced cooperation with the Commission in possession of a right of veto. After the authorization, the Council needs to agree. For the policy fields covered in Article 251 EC, assent of the European Parliament is needed as well. One member of the Council can request to refer the matter to the European Council. For later entry by other Member States, a decision by the Commission is necessary.

2 Four theses

2.1 In advance

Until now, the provisions concerning flexibility have not yet functioned in practice, not even under the Treaty of Amsterdam. This means that it is only a concept on paper at the moment, with which many strategies in practice will be possible. It is therefore impossible to discuss the influence of flexibility on the institutional balance as it will take place when a plea is made to the relevant provisions. Only general observations can be made when studying the flexibility provisions and their context in the Treaties. In this study, therefore, four theses will be proven which result from this study of the provisions. The theses are not necessarily interconnected. The first two theses have a general nature; the last two refer to the position of the different institutions opposite each other.

It has to be kept in mind that the subject of study will be limited to the institutional balance as it will function within the system of flexibility, and not on the institutional balance in all (other) policy fields of the European Union and European Community. Still, the institutional balance for other policy fields could very well be affected by the flexibility system. Simultaneously, the systems of flexibility contain not only procedural aspects but also conditional aspects, which prescribe under which conditions the procedures can be started. Both types of aspects need to be considered when the influence on the institutional relations is discussed.

2.2 A shift towards federalization?

From a federal point of view, the flexibility provisions in the Treaty of Amsterdam have given the European Parliament and the Council of Ministers a more marked position as federal institutions. The amendments to it in the Treaty of Nice have strengthened this idea because they include the later entry of non-participating Member States, thus ensuring the inclusion of all Member States in each decision.

This thesis also refers to the composition of the European Parliament and the Council, as well as to their role in the procedures to establish and implement enhanced cooperation. The European Parliament consists of 'representatives of the peoples of the States brought together in the Community' (Article 189 EC); the Council consists of 'a representative of each Member State at ministerial level, authorized to commit the government of that Member State' (Article 203 EC). For the application of the flexibility provisions, all members of the European Parliament have the right to vote. This is the case in the procedure to establish enhanced cooperation and in the already existing legislative procedures which are used in these new systems. In contrast, only those members of the Council have the right to vote whose governments participate in the project in case of acts and decisions necessary for the implementation of flexible cooperation.

This relation between the European Parliament and the Council is, for instance, easily comparable to the relation between the *Bundesrat* and the *Bundestag* in Germany. These two federal parliaments represent different aspects of federal representation: the *Bundesrat* represents the governments of the *Länder*, whereas the *Bundestag* represents the people of the federation.[11]

This comparison shows that it can easily be said that the positions of the European Parliament and the Council in the flexibility procedures grow towards more federally recognizable positions because, more and more, they begin to occupy similar positions. Moreover, the link with the decision-making procedures from the first pillar contributes to this effect, because these procedures have become more and more federal over the years - when one looks for instance to the co-decision-making procedure - with a better defined role of the European Parliament and a non-unanimity for the Council in many cases. Still, a movement in the direction of federalization does not mean that a federal structure exists or will soon exist, which would stimulate a more democratic structure.

---

[11] F.A.N.J. Goudappel, *Powers and Control Mechanisms in European Federal Systems*, Deventer, 1997, p. 30.

2.3 A shift away from federalization?

The differences in application of flexibility in the first and third pillars gives rise to a moving away from federalization because of the difference in position of Council and Commission in these first and third pillars.

This thesis appears to be contradictory to the first one. The reason for this is that they focus on different elements of the flexibility provisions and on the possible future role these provisions may play. This second thesis focuses on the position of the Council and the Commission opposite each other.

Since the second and third pillar of the European Union were created in the Treaty of Maastricht, it could be observed that these two represented mainly a development in the direction of a confederation (intergovernmental) while also containing elements of a development in the direction of a federation: In the direction of a federation because new policy fields were brought under the European umbrella by the second and third pillar; in the direction of a confederation because in the second and third pillar lay a strong emphasis on the role of the Council in which the Member States had to decide unanimously. This latter aspect appears to be the most influential one, so that the European Union can be said to be mostly intergovernmental. The first pillar, on the other hand, contains the already existing European Community which is often considered to be a federation-to-be, and which thus contains many federal elements.[12] For flexibility, the possibilities in the third pillar appear to be more numerous than in the first pillar, in which the procedure laid down in Article 11 EC may limit the application. Thus, for enhanced cooperation, the confederate elements are stronger than the federal ones.

2.4 The Council and the Commission

A two-step initiative as reflected in the procedure for flexibility in the first pillar does not lead to a better structuring of the relations between the Council of Ministers and the Commission.

The procedure for the establishment of closer cooperation differs for the Council and the Commission in one important aspect. Article 11 EC, prescribes what can be labelled a 'two-step initiative': first, the Member States in the Council have to decide by qualified majority whether they want to request enhanced cooperation in a certain policy field. This Council initiative in the form of a request, however, means that it has decided to propose to the Commission to initiate the necessary process, which forms the right of initiative of the Commission. Thus, both the Council and the Commission exercise some form of initiative, which leads to confusion about the position of each of them because

12 *Ibid*, p. 347-405.

these initiatives have to be performed more or less simultaneously. Because no institution holds a monopoly position on the initiative in this new procedure, the relationship between Council and Commission changes or at least becomes confused.

In addition, the Commission is in a relatively weak position in the procedure in the third pillar. In this flexible cooperation procedure, it mostly has an advisory role. Where the first pillar prescribes authorization by the Commission, the third pillar leaves the Commission with not much more than a formal right of initiative and the presenting of its opinion. In its relation with the Council, this new development towards a stronger position of the Council represents a step towards intergovernmentalism instead of supranationalism because the Council, as such, basically represents the Member States and often decides with unanimity, an expression of intergovernmentalism. Moreover, as already stated above, it is to be expected that the procedure in the third pillar will be followed more often than the one in the first pillar because of the restrictive conditions in the first pillar. This means that a move towards the flexibility procedure in the third pillar is to be expected and thus towards intergovernmentalism.

2.5 The European Parliament

The elimination of the cooperation procedure and the simplification of the co-decision procedure has led to a stronger position of the European Parliament in general. However, this effect could be counterbalanced by the introduction of flexibility procedures.

In this thesis, a connection is made between general developments since the Treaty of Amsterdam concerning the legislative procedures, and the introduction of the flexibility procedures. In view of the subject of institutional balance in general, progress has been made in the Treaty of Amsterdam by changing and simplifying the co-decision procedure and by the elimination of the cooperation procedure in the first pillar.[13] This is generally acclaimed to be an improvement on the strength of the position of the European Parliament because of the removal of the third reading and because of the (negative) final say it has in the co-decision procedure and thus the co-legislative role it has in it.[14] In addition, the European Parliament has a much weaker position in the second and third pillar, in which the emphasis is laid on intergovernmentalism and the position of the Council. Thus, the institutional balance[15] in the European Community and European Union benefits from the changes in the decision-

---

[13] R. Barents, *Het Verdrag van Amsterdam*, Deventer, 1997, p. 90-92.

[14] *Ibid*, p. 92-98.

[15] Considering the view on institutional balance as something which must be gained in future, not as describing the status quo.

making procedures, specifically from the improvement of the position of the European Parliament.

As already stated above, the competencies of the institutions differ in each of the flexibility procedures, which are mostly based on the normal legislative procedures of the first pillar. The procedure in the third pillar especially complicates matters, not only because it is complementary to the general flexibility conditions as laid down in Article 43 EU, but also because the ratios of votes in the Council have to be re-calculated for each case since the Member States which participate in each instance of closer cooperation, will often differ. This means that the position of the European Parliament, which is already relatively weak in the third pillar, suffers from the introduction of the flexibility procedures because of the possible frequency of its application. In the first pillar, however, the position of the European Parliament has been strengthened in comparison to the procedure as it was laid down in the Treaty of Amsterdam. Now, the assent of the European Parliament has been made necessary in all flexibility procedures in Article 251 EC policy fields.

3 Concluding remarks

In conclusion, it has to be observed that it is very likely that not much attention can have been paid to the influence of the flexibility provisions on the institutional balance when the Treaty of Amsterdam was created. The system of flexibility, as such, appears to have been the main aim, and therefore only already existing legislative procedures have been used whilst the differences in position between the institutions in the first and third pillars have been maintained and even strengthened. In the Treaty of Nice, flexibility received special attention and thus some of these developments were limited in their application. Instituting flexibility is now only a last resort, for instance.

When the restrictive conditions and the relevant legislative procedures are being considered in connection with each other, it results in possibly unforeseen changes in the institutional balance because of the flexibility procedures. Each new treaty leads to a new institutional balance, but in this case the flexibility procedures lead to a kind of specific balance for flexibility only. The cases in which enhanced cooperation is allowed by the Treaties and the procedures prescribed in the first and the third pillar give rise to minor and major shifts. The changes lead, for instance, to a shift both towards and away from federalization because the European institutions represent the European Union and the Member States to differing extents. Simultaneously, the position of the European Parliament changes opposite the position of Council and Commission. On top, the positions of the Commission and the Council change opposite each other.

CHAPTER X

Flexibility and the Acquis Communautaire

prof. dr. Elies Steyger

1 Introduction

The Treaty of the European Union, as concluded in Amsterdam in 1997, introduced for the first time explicitly a flexibility-clause in the European Community. This does not mean, however, that with the explicit introduction the opportunity for flexibility in the Community a completely new aspect of community law came into being. Flexibility has been around for a while now, and seems to become one of the more important features in the European legal landscape. It takes on various forms, from opting-out clauses with regard to social policy and the Euro, to protocols to which Member States can accede to at wish.[1] Whether this Europe of bits and pieces is a desirable concept remains to be seen.[2]

The introduction of a flexibility clause by the Treaty of Amsterdam in the EC Treaty itself (Article 11 and after Nice Article 11 *juncto* 11a EC *juncto* 43 EU) may however be the most remarkable appearance of all forms of flexibility. It enables the Member States, after being authorised by the Council in a qualified majority vote, to make use of the Community Institutions and procedures to adopt measures with which the Member States concerned speed up the integration process. This flexibility clause which will be slightly altered by the Treaty of Nice as drafted in February 2001, will be my main focus of attention.

In this contribution I will discuss the three main elements of Article 11 EC as introduced by the Treaty of Amsterdam. I will comment at the limits embedded in the article, especially those which affect the extent to which flexibility is supposed to be applied. Furthermore, I will discuss the question whether the *acquis communautaire* will be affected. Finally I will turn my attention to some practical consequences the article may have. As far as necessary, I will address the changes in the flexibility clause the Treaty of Nice will bring in the near future.

2 The limits of Article 11 EC and Articles 40-44a EU

The original flexibility clause as laid down in Article 11 EC did not provide the Member States with an unlimited freedom to pursue flexible integration. The article itself contained no fewer than five limits for its use, under which free movement and trade restrictions. The first limit to its scope was that the measures taken by the Member State should be within the competence of the Community as allocated by the EC Treaty. Secondly, Member States

---

1 For an overview see among others C.D. Ehlermann, "Différation, flexibilité, coopération renforcée: les nouvelles dispositions du Traité d'Amsterdam", *Revue du Marché Unique Européen*, 3/1997, p. 53-89.

2 D. Curtin, "The Constitutional Structure of the Union. A Europe of bits and pieces", *CMLRev*, 1993, p. 17-69.

were not supposed to pursue flexible integration in those areas belonging to the exclusive jurisdiction of the Community. The revised flexibility clause in the Treaty of Nice encompasses the same limits (Article 43 EU to which Article 11 EC refers).

These two limits alone provide enough source for confusion[3] as to what is actually possible on the basis of Article 11 EC. With that I do not mean to say that those limits should be considered unreasonable. It is not an unreasonable demand that the EC Treaty itself should be respected. Obviously the EC Treaty can not empower the Council to authorise anything which is beyond its scope. If it did, the flexibility clause would automatically lead to an extension of the powers of the Community. Said confusion stems from the fact that the scope of the EC Treaty is not that well defined. This has been demonstrated extensively over the years in several surprise judgements of the Court of Justice in, for example measures concerning administrative law, never mentioned in the Treaty at all.[4] As a result of this ill-defined scope, the extent of the measures for which the Member States can make use of the institutional and procedural framework of the Treaty is equally unclear.

The second limit can cause even a greater problem. The question of which areas belong to the exclusive jurisdiction of the Community is one which has led to severely diverging opinions among academics, not to mention the Community Institutions themselves. To be sure, no serious attempt has been made to interpret the concept of 'exclusive jurisdiction'. This makes it all the more difficult to decide whether the jurisdiction of the Community must be seen as exclusive or not.

For example: the question of whether the internal market belongs to the exclusive jurisdiction of the Community is still open to debate. It has been raised when the principle of subsidiarity (Article 5 EC) was inserted in the EC Treaty by the Treaty of Maastricht in 1993. The principle of subsidiarity also is not applicable in areas belonging to the exclusive jurisdiction of the Community.

In the then ongoing discussion the Commission held the view that the internal market falls within the exclusive jurisdiction of the Community. The Commission interprets 'exclusive jurisdiction' as follows: once the Community has the power to decide the framework within which the Member States are

---

3 Ehlermann *o.c.* also quotes the limit on the distortion of competition as a serious source of confusion. I tend to agree with him, but will not go into it, and refer to his above mentioned contribution to the RMUE for more information.

4 There are many of them in many fields; I confine myself here by referring only to the judgements with regard to the legal protection of individuals in which the Court assumed that all kinds of implicit obligations follow from Article 11 EC. See among others: S. Prechal, *Directives in European Community Law,* Oxford, 1995, 148-187, E. Steyger, R.J.G.M. Widdershoven, A.W.H. Meij, *Europees recht en het Nederlands bestuursrecht,* Alphen a/d de Rijn, 1996, p. 50-61 and 126-148.

allowed to act, the jurisdiction is exclusive. This is the case even when the Member States do have a considerable latitude to act within that framework, so long as the Community has not taken harmonising measures. I agree with the Commission on its concept of exclusivity.[5] In my view a power allocated by the Treaty is exclusive, if eventually the Community is empowered to override the remaining powers of the Member States. This applies to the power to take exception as well as to the power to redefine those remaining national powers.

However, this is a point of view contested, among others, by the legal service of the Council and in legal literature. Schrauwen for example maintains that the powers of the Community with regard to the internal market are not exclusive.[6] Since the Member States are still able to take exception and are entitled within the framework of the articles establishing the internal market to adopt protective measures as long as harmonisation has not taken place, she feels the powers between the Member States and the Community are shared.

Schrauwen and I do not differ in our respective opinions as to what the Member States still are entitled to regulate or decide and to what extent they are allowed to do so. Our differences apply only to the question of what we regard to be 'exclusive'. In my opinion a power is not exclusive any more once another administration is entitled to define its limits. As I understand it, in Schrauwens opinion a power is not exclusive as long as other administrations are entitled to take the measures they deem necessary and can only be overruled through an act of that other administration.

If Schrauwens opinion is correct not many exclusive powers are allocated to the Community. For example: since the *IJssel-Vliet* case, one may even wonder whether powers such as the Community has with regard to state aid may be called exclusive.[7] In *IJssel-Vliet* the Court of Justice ruled that policy rules designed to clarify the use of the powers of the Commission with regard to the application of Article 87 EC should be accepted by the Member States as a part of the cooperation between the Member States and the Community. Whether that acceptance must be seen as a constituting factor for the validity of these policy rules remains unclear. The fact that the necessity of acceptance of the policy rules by the Member States was emphasised by the Court may point at a shared competence in the matter. If acceptance is a constituting factor, the powers of the Community can not be seen as exclusive.

---

5 E. Steyger, *Europe and its members, A Constitutional Approach*, Dartmouth, 1995, at p. 68-72.

6 A. Schrauwen, *Marché intérieur, Recherches sur une notion*, Amsterdam, 1997; see also A. Mattera, *Le marche unique européen, ses regles, son fonctionnement*, Paris, 1990, who regards the opportunity for member states to take exception for non-economic reasons to Article 30 as the core of their exclusive powers left to them.

7 Case C-311/94 *Ijssel-Vliet Combinatie v. Minister van Economische Zaken* [1996] ECR I-5023.

According to the Treaty of Amsterdam, the extent of the EC-Treaty as such, and the definition of 'exclusive jurisdiction' would have been the first problem which should be dealt with, with regard to the flexibility-clause. These problems have not been solved by the Treaty of Nice.

Also another problem relating to flexibility is still very much there. That is the problem how flexibility relates to the *acquis communautaire.*

3 Does flexibility in the EC Treaty affect the acquis communautaire?

The main element which has always been emphasised with regard to the subject of closer cooperation is the understanding that the *acquis communautaire* must not be affected. This was also one of the limitations embedded in the original Article 11 EC as inserted by the Treaty of Amsterdam. The Treaty of Nice inserts this same limit in the Treaty of the European Union (Article 43) to which Article 11 of the EC Treaty refers. However, is it possible that the use of the procedures to achieve flexibility does not affect the *acquis communautaire*? If so, what then is the additional value of Article 11 of the Treaty of Amsterdam, or Article 43 EU.

Legally there is no need for a flexibility-clause in the Treaty. Agreements between the Member States to speed up the integration process without violating the *acquis communautaire* never have been inconsistent with the Treaty at all. This is still the case for agreements which are not the result of the use of the procedures of the flexibility-clause. Even the question of whether such an action does fall within the exclusive jurisdiction (in whatever sense that term must be interpreted) is of no concern, as long as the *acquis communautaire* is left in peace. The contents of the Treaty itself, as specifically embedded in Article 43(c) and (e) EU Treaty, define the limits as to what is possible for Member States which want closer cooperation.

With that in mind it is arguable that Articles 11 and 11a EC *juncto* Article 43 EU, do not serve any real purpose. It only introduces bureaucratic procedures for aims which can be achieved anyway. Since flexibility is explicitly incorporated in the Treaty, however, I tend to think it should serve a certain purpose.

Flexibility will affect the *acquis communautaire* once it is going to be used. The reason behind that thought is the following. The measures taken in closer cooperation will serve a purpose of which the cooperating Member States think is of a high interest. Once the closer cooperation is achieved, it is reasonable that the cooperating states will defend this interest. This defence will not just affect third countries, but will also be mounted against other EC Member States, who do not or cannot participate in the group of Member States which achieved the closer cooperation. The consequence of this defensive attitude may be that the effects of the measures subject to closer cooperation exceed the effects of measures following from EC law itself. This somewhat cryptic description will become clear once it is illustrated by the following example.

Let us assume that a certain number of Member States decide that they are going to establish a closer cooperation with regard to certain environmental measures such as an increased reduction of air- or water-pollution. The environment is an area known to fall within the jurisdiction of the Community, but certainly does not belong to the Community's exclusive jurisdiction. Even if the core of the measures adopted, only affect the environment as such, it is to be expected that a spill-over effect of the measures concerned ensues. This spill-over effect may well lead to certain requirements concerning the composition or the packaging of goods already existing in the closer cooperating Member States. Also the way transborder services are provided may be affected. For example requirements concerning an environmental friendly way to provide the service, or a certain amount of additional knowledge of the service provider may be introduced.

If these spill-over effects lead to additional provisions in the closer cooperation agreement, necessary to achieve the purpose of the closer cooperation, the closer cooperation in itself may lead to harsher requirements on goods or services provided from non-participating Member States. If the non-participating Member States cannot comply with the new requirements, eventually they may see the borders of the cooperating states closed for their products and services. If the cooperating Member States would not close their borders, the purpose of the closer cooperation might become obsolete. Thus certain products and services which may have been at the market for years, suddenly could be denied free circulation in the Community. In such a case, the *acquis communautaire i.e.* the free movement of goods or services is most definitely affected.

Proper doctrine would say that measures introducing additional requirements for goods or services either cannot be adopted or must be completely in concordance with the EC Treaty. Otherwise they are violating Community law. However, authorised by the Council to take measures with the purpose to improve the environment, the closer cooperating Member States most likely will protest such an interpretation. Obviously, said interpretation would undermine the interests for which the closer cooperation was started in the first place. As a consequence, they most probably would invoke Article 30 EC or the rule of reason in the case of goods, the Articles 55 *juncto* 46 EC in the case of services to stop the offending goods to enter their territory or the offending services to be provided. The result is a restriction in trade.

The above requires some nuances. The Articles 30 or 55 *juncto* 46 EC, as well as the rule of reason, can only be invoked by the closer cooperating Member States, as long as no harmonisation at the Community level has taken place. This is long standing case law[8], and there is no reason to assume it will be different

8 For Article 30 EC see Case 148/78 *Ratti* [1980] ECR 2299; for the rule of reason see Joined Cases 3,4 and 6/76 *Kramer* [1976] ECR 1279.

when certain Member States will decide to use the procedures embedded in Article 11. Thus, in case no harmonisation has taken place, the only new element the flexibility clause would bring is that products or services already freely circulating may be banned from the market of the closer cooperating Member States because of the cooperation agreement. For new products or services, nothing changes. If not measuring up to the standards of either other Member States in general or the closer cooperating ones, it may face a ban on the grounds of either Article 30 EC, the rule of reason or Article 55 *juncto* 46 EC. So again, Article 11 (as Articles 11a EC and Article 43 EU) does not seem to add much to the existing possibilities pre-Amsterdam. So what is left is the question: what do Article 11 EC *juncto* Article 43 EU add? And that could be of course that the closer cooperating Member States may be allowed to invoke the exceptions of the Treaty or the ones laid down in case-law, after national law is harmonised at the Community level.

Even though the wording of the Articles 11a EC and Article 43(e) EU suggest that an interpretation allowing the Member States to invoke Article 30 or 55 *juncto* 46 EC is impossible, one may wonder whether that is true. There is another element to be considered here, a constitutional element to be precise. The fact that measures taken according to the procedures of Articles 11 and 11a do have their own basis in the EC Treaty and must be authorised by the Council before adoption, does have a certain significance. That significance is twofold.

Firstly, unless the participating Member States adopt measures which are clearly not included in the Council authorisation, the measures taken in closer cooperation must be regarded valid. This is the case, even when they do have a spill-over effect as described above. As a consequence the measures taken in closer cooperation become part of Community law itself! The result is that two measures of Community law: the exceptions from the EC Treaty as laid down in the treaty-articles and the case-law on the rule of reason on the one hand, and the measures taken in closer cooperation on the other are incompatible. Since in a legal landscape order needs to be maintained, incompatible measures must be interpreted so as to become compatible.

The Treaty of Nice (in Article 44, (1) last sentence EU) aims to resolve this dilemma by stating that the decisions made in closer cooperation do not become part of the *acquis* of the Union. It is not clear what this sentence means. If it does mean that decisions made in closer cooperation are not part of Community law, a legal oddity occurs. In that case a Council-authorisation, based on a power allocated in the Treaty would not only be part of Community law, itself; arguable then is that the legal procedures embedded in the Treaty, such as appeal against the withholding of the authorisation would not be applicable. It is hardly imaginable that that is the case. So the probable meaning of the sentence of Article 44 EU is, that other Member States cannot rely on the measures taken in closer cooperation as if they were part of the acquis. But that does not change their status of being Community law.

Secondly, since the measures are adopted according to the prescribed procedures, the Court of Justice may judge their validity primarily against the question whether the measures exceed the authority given by the Council and whether the authorisation itself is within the limits of the EC Treaty. As long as the authorisation itself can be considered valid, and the measures taken are within this authorisation, they probably will be regarded as compatible with Community law. The only criterion then is whether either the authorisation or the measures are *ultra vires*. This kind of examination, which in The Netherlands is called marginal testing, because only the margins of the regulatory measure are taken into consideration, respects the latitude the legislator is allocated. It is not an uncommon way to examine the activities of the legislator against rules of a higher value in continental legal systems.

If these two assumptions are correct, the measures taken in closer cooperation must be regarded as a *lex specialis* in relation to measures taken by the Community as a whole. On the one hand they are part of Community law. Moreover, they are subject to an authorisation procedure of the Council, which follows from the Treaty itself. They are as much based on a Treaty article and subjected to procedures incorporated in the Treaty as the general harmonisation-measures at Community level itself. The only way to avoid problems with two valid regulatory measures applicable to the same subject matter at the same time, is to apply the *lex specialis* doctrine. That way incompatibility is avoided.

If the *lex specialis* doctrine is applicable, one may even wonder whether the need for invoking the Articles 30 or 55 *juncto* 46 EC is there at all. In that case the closer cooperation measure will prevail anyway, so the Community measure simply is not to be applied. But presumably the opportunity to invoke the exceptions to the free movement of goods and services must be open in case of doubt. Also, otherwise Articles 11 EC *juncto* 43 EU would not serve any purpose, other than providing more bureaucratic procedures for actions which have been compatible with the EC Treaty from its very first beginning. Thus, the mere fact of the incorporation of the procedure for closer cooperation will affect the *acquis communautaire* as we know it.

I do believe, however, that the *acquis communautaire* may be threatened even more seriously, because of the practical implications of flexibility.

4 The implications of flexibility for the application of Community law in practice

The above indicates that it is hard to incorporate flexible cooperation between Member States in the structure of Community law, without doing serious harm to the application of the law. As said this is partly due to the structure of Community law as interpreted by the Court of Justice. Additionally a more practical problem must be faced: the effects of closer cooperation on the application of the law by the executing authorities.

Community law, and more in particular the secondary law and the case-law of the Court of Justice, is already fairly complicated to apply in concrete situations. It is not uncommon that national authorities make mistakes while applying decisions of the Commission. It is quite difficult for non-specialised national authorities to catch up with the 'do's and don'ts' of Community law as promulgated by the various institutions. The practical side of the application of Community law should therefore get some more attention of the Community legislator than it has today.

With closer cooperation, on top of the existing legislation, a new kind of measures will appear, which will be applicable to only a certain number of Member States and only in a number of specified situations. They are added to the already existing number of differently applicable laws following either from Community law or from national law. Do we really expect the executing authorities keep up with their obligations to apply all that without making mistakes?

It is well known, that authorities, which can not keep up with the law they are supposed to apply, often apply the law they know and can keep up with. That law is not necessarily the law which is valid. What I am trying to say here is something not always appreciated by lawyers, and seldom acknowledged by academics: if Community law, because of the opportunities for flexibility, becomes more complicated than it already is, its application as a whole is seriously threatened.

Complicating the law through the closer cooperation clause in the EC Treaty may constitute a more serious danger for the *acquis communautaire* then the negotiators of the Treaties of Amsterdam and Nice may have realised. They did not take the limits of executing authorities into account. And do not think that the legal protection against the actions of those authorities as required by the Court will be enough to safeguard Community law. Of course individuals are able to appeal against decisions and rely on the law which is valid. They can force the executing authorities to uphold the appropriate law in specific situations. However, will the citizens always be able to know which law is applicable? Will the legal practitioners be able enough? And thus, even if the (national) judges manage to keep up with the ever changing law, there will be too few appeals to change the practice of not-knowing. So the risk to the *acquis communautaire* is that the use of Articles 11a EC *juncto* 43 EU eventually 'flexibilises' that same *acquis* into obscurity. Therefore alone closer cooperation under Articles 11 EC *juncto* 43 EU should be kept at an absolute minimum.

5 Some closing remarks

For quite a while now, Europe has had a tendency to achieve its unity by catering to many Member States' whims. The result is an unreadable EU Treaty with many protocols containing opting-out clauses, special treatment clauses, and other bits and pieces which do not convey the impression of a strong Union, growing towards its goals. Maybe unity in Europe cannot be achieved any other way. The inclusion of the flexibility-clause has as its purpose the integration within the European Union. But the legal as well as practical problems deriving from a frequent use of the clause may actually undermine the integration of Europe as a whole. Therefore the Council, who will be the guardian of the clause, has a big responsibility to apply the authorisation procedure as careful as possible.

CHAPTER XI

Sovereignty Revisited

Margreth H.M. de Bonth

1 Sovereignty: a threat to integration

In the 1960's, the European Court of Justice announced the beginning of the end of state sovereignty for the Member States. In two famous cases, *Van Gend & Loos* and *Costa-ENEL*, the Court decided that the Member States 'have limited their sovereign rights, albeit within limited fields',[1] and that this 'limitation of their sovereign rights' is 'permanent'.[2] Ever since, any invocation of sovereignty has been regarded as a motion of distrust, and therefore as a threat to the integration process. However, an alternative approach to the notion of sovereignty may lead to a different conclusion.

The notion of sovereignty is dynamic. It was first formulated by Jean Bodin in 1576.[3] At that time, it was embodied in the person of the Sovereign, the most striking example of which was King Louis XIV of France. In 1681, John Locke introduced the notion of popular sovereignty in his *Two Treatises of Government*. The 19th century marked the transition to depersonalization of the notion of sovereignty. The state as an independent legal entity became the bearer of sovereignty, and it is this notion of state sovereignty that we are still talking about. The essence of the notion is very much interwoven with the power structures, which means that changes in power structures are reflected in the interpretation of the notion of sovereignty. Even if the word 'sovereignty' were to be replaced, the essence of the notion would not change. The European Union represents a new power structure that is unique in its kind. Especially in the context of the European integration process, the notion of sovereignty has its value explaining the underlying power structure.

In order to show the value of the notion of sovereignty in the European Union, it is necessary to make a distinction between 'negative' and 'positive' sovereignty. This distinction comes from the German legal scholar Georg Jellinek.[4] In his view, 'negative' sovereignty refers to the notion that the state as a sovereign entity holds the superior power on its territory. No other superior power is tolerated, and thus no legal limitations can be imposed on the state against its will. More important but hardly discussed with respect to the European Union is the notion of 'positive' sovereignty. According to Jellinek, this means that states can use their sovereign power to limit themselves.

---

* I wish to thank Anna-Miria Mühlke and Susanne Himstedt for their valuable comments on earlier drafts.

1 Case 26/62 *Van Gend en Loos* [1963] ECR 1.

2 Case 6/64 *Costa v. ENEL* [1964] ECR 585.

3 J. Bodin, *Les Six Livres de la République*, Scientia Verlag Aalen, 1977, second reprint of the 1583 Paris edition. See also J.H. Franklin, *Jean Bodin: On Sovereignty*, Cambridge, 1992.

4 G. Jellinek, *Allgemeine Staatslehre*, Kronberg, 1976, third edition, p.453-482.

It is a justified exercise of their power. Nevertheless, sovereignty in the European Union is usually linked with unanimity, veto power and obstruction of integration and clearly refers to the notion of 'negative' sovereignty.

The emphasis on the notion of 'negative' sovereignty has caused confusion. As a consequence, the threat of national sovereignty to the European integration process has been exaggerated. By focusing on the notion of 'negative' sovereignty, the European Union has embarked on an ostrich policy with respect to the notion of sovereignty. Hiding behind a veil of integration is not only unnecessary but also undesirable. The structure of the European Union is such that it cannot exist without the sovereignty of the Member States. It is a fiction that the invocation of sovereignty within the European Union actually threatens the integration process. In fact, the use of sovereignty by the Member States should be viewed in a much more positive way. More honesty about the sovereignty of the Member States might help in clarifying the position of the Member States vis-a-vis the European Union. For instance, for the outside world it is important to know with whom they are dealing. Furthermore potential new Member States might want to know in familiar terminology what their position will be when they enter the European Union, and public support from the European citizens may be higher when the question of national sovereignty is addressed adequately.

I will show that the European Union exists by virtue of the sovereignty of its Member States. Their sovereignty not only forms the basis of the integration process, but is also the motor behind the ever closer cooperation. Instead of a loss of sovereignty by the transfer of sovereign rights to the European Union, it is in the process of limitation that their sovereignty becomes more apparent. It is time to let go of the negative connotations that have haunted the notion of sovereignty for almost four centuries. We have to start focusing on the positive use states can make of their sovereignty. The most expressive example is their cooperation within the European Union.

2 Flexibility as an expression of sovereignty

The Treaty of Amsterdam has given a new impulse to the discussion about the sovereignty of the Member States. By introducing the notion of *flexibility* or *enhanced cooperation*, the Member States have been accused of safeguarding their own competencies within the Treaty.[5] *Flexibility* creates the possibility for some Member States to cooperate more closely in specific areas within the European Union. This practice is not new. It has already been used in the Schengen agreement, and it will also be used in the Economic and

[5] W. Sauter, "The Economic Constitution of the European Union", 4 *Columbia Journal of European Law*, Winter/Spring, 1998, p. 35.

Monetary Union. Unlike in the Schengen agreement, the concept of *flexibility* in the Treaties of Amsterdam and Nice means that these activities will take place within the framework of the European Union.[6]

The introduction of the notion of *flexibility* brings in the sovereignty paradox. On the one hand, the Member States seem to retain their sovereignty with respect to cooperation in some fields. On the other hand, the Member States accept to limit themselves by agreeing on this procedure within the framework of the European Union.

3 The sovereignty paradox: 'In der Beschränkung zeigt sich erst die Souveränität'

The paradox *'In der Beschränkung zeigt sich erst die Souveränität'*[7] can be explained by using the distinction made by Georg Jellinek between 'negative' and 'positive' sovereignty. Discussions about sovereignty in the European Union focus on 'negative' sovereignty. Main issues are the transfer of sovereign rights by the Member States to the European Union and a corresponding loss of sovereignty. Great Britain is notorious for the invocation of its sovereignty. France also has a history of using the sovereignty argument, the best example being the Luxembourg Compromise of 1966. Another famous example is the first Danish 'no' to the Maastricht Treaty. The European Court of Justice refers to 'negative' sovereignty when stating that the Member States have limited their sovereign rights permanently. These well-known examples all reflect the notion of 'negative' sovereignty. Yet, far more fundamental are the innumerable occasions where they have made a positive use of their sovereignty.

The possible loss of sovereignty invokes fear and suspicion in the Member States, but in fact the Member States have not lost their sovereignty by creating the European Union. Sovereignty is indivisible and is more than just the sum of sovereign rights. The Member States have been able to construct the European Union because they are sovereign states. They expressed their sovereign will by taking decisions on the transfer of sovereign rights and chose to limit their sovereignty, making a positive use of their sovereignty. Since sovereignty is indivisible, loss of sovereignty cannot be measured. This can best be illustrated by an example.

Switzerland is not a member of the European Union. It is often pictured as being more sovereign than the Member States of the European Union. Switzerland is a close trading partner of the European Union and relies heavily

---

6 See especially the contribution of Elies Steyger in this volume, Chapter X.

7 Taken from the expression by Johann Wolfgang von Goethe: 'In der Beschränkung zeigt sich erst der Meister' (It is self-limitation that reveals a true master), Sonett: Natur und Kunst.

on the European Union for its exports. In order to export to the European Union, Switzerland has to comply with the so-called *acquis communautaire*. The *acquis communautaire* contains all the rules and regulations agreed on by the Member States. Yet, Switzerland did not have any say in the establishment of these rules. How sovereign is a country like Switzerland in that respect? This is not to say that the Member States of the European Union are necessarily more sovereign than Switzerland. Again, sovereignty cannot be measured. The Swiss example puts sovereignty in the European Union in a different perspective. Sovereignty is always relative.

4 Limitations of absolute sovereignty

The Swiss example leads us to rethink the notion of sovereignty. All too often sovereignty is presented as absolute. If sovereignty means complete independence from other countries, then not a single country in the world can be fully sovereign. In this era of globalization and interdependence every state relies on other states, especially when it comes to trade.

It is common to make a distinction between internal and external sovereignty. They represent two sides of the same coin. The Swiss example illustrates the notion of external sovereignty, independence from other sovereign states. Internal sovereignty deals with the exclusive state powers within a certain territory, not allowing any higher authority. In the context of the European Union both the internal and external sovereignty of the Member States are affected. The Member States have transferred some of their internal sovereign powers to the European Union. By doing so they have increased their dependence on the other Member States. When we look at sovereignty as being absolute, this could suggest that they have lost part of their sovereignty. But sovereignty is always relative. Whether we are discussing the internal or the external sovereignty of a state, neither one can be perceived as being absolute.

The fiction of absolute power of the sovereign has given the notion of sovereignty a bad name. Mistakenly Jean Bodin is seen as the father of the notion of absolute sovereignty. Bodin himself is not a proponent of the notion of absolute sovereignty. He acknowledges that the power vested in the sovereign can be used and misused. The ultimate power rests with the sovereign, *i.e.* the King. The King is the supreme legislator. Therefore, it is not possible to limit the power of the King with man-made laws. The only limitations and guarantees against the abuse of power are the laws of God and nature. To Bodin, those are very important and strong limitations of the power of the King. While recognising the absolute power of the King in earthly matters, Bodin places great emphasis on the limitations of this power by natural and spiritual laws. Thus, according to Bodin, even the absolute power of the King is limited and relative. Nevertheless, Louis XIV of France, the Sun King, made use of this notion of absolute sovereignty. He legitimised his rule by claiming that he ruled by the grace of God. He abused the power vested in him. The atrocities committed under his reign continue to give the notion of sovereignty the bad name it has today. It is very important to bear in mind that all sovereign power can be used and misused. World history has numerous examples of incidents and wars in which atrocities took place legitimised by an appeal to sovereignty.

In order to contain unrestricted and arbitrary use of power by the sovereign, the history of the notion of sovereignty is filled with different ways of limiting the power of the sovereign. For instance, the internal sovereignty of a modern state is legally limited by its constitution, which regulates the separation of power within the state. With respect to external sovereignty, the most important legal limitation can be found in treaties among states. Treaties are agreements between sovereign states and can be seen as expressions of the sovereign will of states, as expressions of 'positive' sovereignty.

Outside the context of the European Union, treaties are not perceived as infringements on state sovereignty. For instance, when some states conclude a trade agreement, it is not discussed in terms of how this affects their sovereignty. We can use the distinction between 'negative' and 'positive' sovereignty here again. We can say that the states party to the agreement have used their 'positive' sovereignty to limit themselves voluntarily. The *quid pro quo* is that the states party will mutually benefit from this trade agreement. A more institutionalised example is the United Nations. The establishment of the United Nations is also based on a treaty. The Charter of the United Nations explicitly recognises the sovereign equality of states. One could say that the Charter acknowledges the 'positive' sovereignty of states. Loss of sovereignty is not an issue in the UN context. However, these examples clearly show that in many respects sovereignty is always limited and relative.

The European Union is also built on treaties. The European integration process is based on the assumption that closer economic cooperation would be beneficial for all the Member States. In 1951, the Member States entered into the first treaty establishing the European Community of Coal and Steel as sovereign states. This perception changed when the European Court of Justice pronounced itself on the issue of state sovereignty, stating that the Member States had limited their sovereign rights permanently.[8] We can agree with these decisions and still uphold the view that the Member States of the European Union are sovereign. I would even go as far as to say that the use of sovereignty is secured in the structure of the European Union.

---

8 See footnotes 1 and 2.

5 Structural use of sovereignty in the European Union

Despite attempts to restructure the division of power within the European Union, the main decision making body is still the Council of Ministers. Even though the European Commission has some supranational powers and the European Parliament has obtained a more serious role in the legislative process, the European Commission is not a European government, nor is the European Parliament as powerful as its national counterparts. The Council of Ministers consists of representatives of the Member States, who are not independent. They represent the national interests. In terms of sovereignty, every time the Council of Ministers takes a vote, the representatives of the respective Member States make use of their sovereignty. They take a decision to limit their sovereignty. They can only do so because they are sovereign. In return, the current decision making structure also permits the Council of Ministers to reuse some of the sovereign rights they transferred to the European Union, though in a different setting.

Within the framework of the European Union the use of 'negative' sovereignty is contained. The legal limitations are such that it is impossible for one Member State to dominate all the others. This means that abuse of sovereign power is excluded within the framework of the European Union. Opponents of the notion of sovereignty can see this as proof of permanent loss of sovereignty. However, considering the framework of the European Union as an infringement on sovereignty only makes sense from the perspective of 'negative' sovereignty. On the other hand, from the perspective of 'positive' sovereignty, it cannot be viewed as a loss, but as a confirmation of sovereignty. The instances in which Member States have referred to the notion of 'negative' sovereignty are more widely known. Nevertheless, the positive use of sovereignty by the Member States has been prevalent throughout the whole process of integration.

6 The European integration process is unique

Ever since the establishment of the first European Community of Coal and Steel in 1951, the European integration process has been unique. It is unique in comparison to other international organisations, and compared to other federal states. It is not a purely intergovernmental organisation, nor is it a federal state. The degree of cooperation and the willingness to adopt majority decision making in certain fields is greater than in any other international organisation, yet it is not a federal state in the classic sense. The fact that the European Union cannot be classified as one of the familiar existing entities, shows the difficult task of the Member States when creating this organisation. It has been a process of trial and error.

By establishing the first European Community of Coal and Steel in 1951, six years after the end of the Second World War, the Member States more or less signed a peace treaty. We could draw this parallel even further by saying that the following treaties have reinforced this state of peaceful coexistence. At any rate, peace has been the most important result of the integration process. From the beginning, the integration process was designed as a safeguard against the abuse of power. The European Union structure contains the power of the Member States. Although it is rather unique, this framework is yet another limitation of sovereignty.

The notion of sovereignty has survived and evolved during the past four centuries. Sovereignty is a necessary corollary of the European integration process. The current structure of the European Union cannot survive without the sovereignty of the Member States. More clarity with respect to the sovereignty of the Member States is in the best interest of the European Union and the integration process. It may elucidate discussions with the outside world, with prospective Member States, and with the European citizens. We can look at the notion of *flexibility* as another expression of 'positive' sovereignty. Contrary to what critics say, *flexibility* is not a threat to further integration. It is contained within the framework of the European Union, and as an expression of 'positive' sovereignty, *flexibility* is one of the catalytic forces moving the integration process.

CHAPTER XII

Authority or Stability

Flexibility in the Light of Constitutional History

prof. dr. W.T. Eijsbouts

1 L'Europe, roseau réfléchissant*

Lawyers are functional optimists: any weird instrument to come out of the political process they will eventually put to some good use. Thus it will be with the new instrument of flexibility: no doubt some day it will be found to afford the way out of an awkward situation. Then we shall know what it can do.

One may also, however, appreciate the instrument without waiting for its ultimate use: as the result of the show down in Amsterdam, summer 1997. Flexibility in the form it was put down into the Treaties (and subsequently altered in Nice) may be seen as a choice made. The first question then is: which were the options? The second: which of them was adopted? These are the questions inviting the following remarks.

All forms of flexibility in the last instance have been called forth by two opposed trends in the Union's development. The one is that of its growing comprehensiveness, exclusiveness and entwining. The opposite is that of increasing diversity in the Union's membership as to economic development and European political commitment.

The first tendency, the entwining of policy fields and membership, makes the Union special in the international community. Binding forms of cooperation are normally diverse and isolated as to subject matter and participants, which expresses the members' autonomy or sovereignty. This is not so with the Union. No surprise then, the Union's entwining provokes all sorts of internal forms of diversity, down to the core of the Union's legal system: the common (or internal) market. Minimum-harmonisation is a case in point. It indicates common rules or standards that nevertheless leave to committed members the choice of a stricter norm. Another sign is the ineradicable exceptions or safeguards to Union obligations that propagate themselves from primary into secondary legislation of the Union.

One may explain and even conjure these phenomena in part by tackling them piecemeal, but in the last instance they will not disappear, resulting as they do from the lack of a compelling State-structure which would bring about uniformity as a self evident element of the social contract.

The second tendency, of increasing heterogeneity of members with each new enlargement and certainly with the coming one East, has been expressly adduced as a motive for introducing flexibility in the Amsterdam Treaty. In Nice it re-appeared for relaxing the flexibility clauses.

---

* *L' homme n'est qu' un roseau...mais c'est un roseau pensant;* Pascal, pensée 347-200.

That a necessity should be generally felt to reconcile the two trends is not to say that all involved conceive of it in the same terms. Quite to the contrary, even. Which are the opinions? They may be contrasted by placing flexibility in a constitutional and historical perspective and thus undoing it of its new clothes. A preliminary question then arises: do we take a federal or a confederate perspective?

2 Federal systems

A federal system is marked off from a confederate one by the absence in the composing states of important external powers, by their uniform system of administration and by the centralisation of existential and communicative state functions such as defence, diplomacy, police, justice, market and currency.

Enhanced cooperation, the European Union's term for flexibility, is possible between groups of states in a federal system. It is even quite common. In Germany and the US there are all sorts of cooperative schemes, sometimes these are even legally provided for, especially between contingent states. Even in unitary systems such as the Netherlands there are such forms of cooperation. In France you have the *'communauté de communes'*.

These schemes are, however, fundamentally different from the new European Union formula in the fact that they each have their own institutions of cooperation, which remain at the lower level. They do not make use of central instances.

To become comparable to the Union's varieties there would have to be for the states, districts or municipalities the possibility to call in central authority and central institutions, as is provided by Article 43 EU. This sort of instrument is not normally a part of federal nor even unitary systems.

The other side of the same medal is equally hard to imagine in federal systems. It would consist of the possibility for the federated parts to *withdraw* from central authority, institutions, obligations, in certain fields.

In this way the federal model indicates well, albeit *a contrario*, what is the gist of flexibility in the Union. It is cooperation between some members which does not take place at their common level, but at the higher, central, level, and which affects the power balance between the members and the Union. Now this of course can happen either in a regulated or in a non regulated fashion. The European Union Treaty's ambition is mostly to bring such non-regulated forms of partial cooperation affecting the balance, into the harness of the Treaties.[1]

---

1 For the way sub-systems may affect the centre: Philippe de Schoutheete, "The European Community and its sub-systems", in W. Wallace (ed.), *The dynamics of European Integration*, London, 1992.

This means the instrument serves the compelling and exclusive nature of the Union's institution in exchange for a certain permanent freedom of the sub-groups. These are clothed with the authority and given the means of the Union institutions, in return for moulding their initiatives to suit the Union. But they do not point towards a higher degree of federal order.

The true nature of flexibility, as incorporated in the Union Treaties, is better understood from confederate systems than from federal ones.

3 Confederate systems and flexibility

In confederate systems, such as the (first) German Empire (936-1806), the Dutch Republic (1579-1795), the American confederacy (1776-1789), the German confederation (1815-1866) and Switzerland (1355-1848 interrupted by the French period), cooperation of the partners which affects the centre or which even is organised by it, is quite ordinary, even though it is not usually regulated constitutionally. The initial period of the Dutch Republic has striking similarity with that of the Union. The (leading) province of Holland sought close cooperation with Zeeland on the basis of an existing Union between the two from 1576, and with Utrecht. Jonathan Israel writes: 'Priority was given to negotiating with Utrecht as part of what we might term the inner confederate bloc of the three to which the outlying provinces would have no choice but to subordinate themselves.'[2] The provinces of Overijssel, Gelderland and Groningen at first did not even get a seat in the Council of State.[3]

The Dutch inner core brought authority and cohesion to the Republic and would ultimately help to bring about unity. This is what is expected to happen in the Union context as well, as one may read in the well-known piece by Schäuble and Lamers of 1994, in which they put forward the idea of a 'hard core'.[4]

---

2 *The Dutch Republic. Its Rise, Greatness, and Fall 1477-1806*, Oxford, 1995, p. 217.

3 The denomination 'province' derives from the status which these territorial units had in the Burgundian state, from which they ended up under Spanish domination, against which they fought their independence.

4 CDU/CSU-Fraktion des Deutschen Bundestages *Überlegungen zur Europapolitik*, Bonn, 1.Sept. 1994. See *Europe/Documents* 1895/94, 7/9/1994: 'In addition to ensuring that the decision-making process within the European Union becomes more efficient and democratic, the existing hard core of countries oriented to greater integration and closer co-operation must be further strengthened. At present, the core comprises five or six countries. This core must not be closed to other member states; rather, it must be open to every member state willing and able to meet its requirements.'

How this is expected to happen is indeed demonstrated in the Republic, where obstinate members where forced by others back onto the right path.[5]

Government under such conditions is not a gentle affair. It requires the use of coalitions against the unwilling partners and even the threat or use of violence against them. Such 'flexibility' is, then, another word for the motto of the Roman Senate in its traffic with the neighbouring powers: *divide et impera*. Now is this a promise for the Union?

It is a condition for such a system to be workable that there should be one partner that clearly dominates, to manage the coalitions, as in the Republic the province of Holland. For a modern version one may look at NATO under American leadership, or Russia in the CIS, which draws the other participants into changing coalitions of which only itself is invariably a member, so that it can call the tune.

This model we shall call the 'authoritative' model, as it manages to generate authority out of a relatively loose set of partner-countries. The Republic was, in fact, a major player in the European world in spite of its internal divisions.

The authoritative model of flexibility is implicit in the Union's traditional terminology, such as in expressions of multi-speed, *plusieurs vitesses*. The metaphors picked from cycling races point to different groups of contestants who will each arrive at the same finish line, with those in the lead challenging the others to greater speed. The same model is implicit in metaphors such as a caravan or a convoy, as a whole on the way to a single destination and kept together by the captain and by the fear of otherwise becoming a lone prey to pirates.[6]

Above, I argued that the Dutch Republic in its formative stage bears some striking resemblance to the Union of today. But there is a great difference as well. In the Republic one of the territorial entities, the province of Holland, dominated. This proves to be a decisive difference. Situations where there is no single dominating entity are fully different. Jonathan Israel in his quoted book on the Republic, notes a contrasting weakness in the Spanish Netherlands, which he explains from the rivalry between centres of power in the South, notably the cities of the provinces of Brabant and Flanders.

A totally different situation from that in the Dutch Republic will follow from a leadership which is not based on a single party's domination. Take Swiss history. From the creation of the Swiss core, the *Urschwyz* (1355) the

---

5 J.L. Price, *Holland and the Dutch Republic in the Seventeenth Century; The Politics of Particularism*, Oxford, 1994. Price points out how Holland's predominance and authority was maintained through an intricate practice of negotiation, which had little relationship to the formal constitutional structure of the Union of Utrecht.

6 Helmut Kohl said that one ship should not slow down the convoy. *Europe/political day* 6310, 8/9/94 p. 2. H. and W. Wallace use the imagery of a gaggle of geese: *Flying together in a larger and more diverse European Union*, Den Haag, 1995, p. 11.

Swiss Confederation has led a dismal existence. The essence of this system is a complicated balancing act between the different nationalities composing it and between the surrounding states. Always there is the tendency of leagues between part of the cantons or between separate cantons and neighbouring powers. The temptations may be linguistic in origin, as from French, Germanic or Italian neighbour, or religious, as from the Netherlands and Britain after the reformation. It is a feeble system, finding its strength in its weakness and in the jealousy of the neighbours.

Then Napoleon disrupts the balance, creating the Helvetian Republic, a sort of unitary state. This does not last, as Napoleon is even forced to restore the cantons, but the liberal cantons have smelled modernity and create their own league. As an answer, the old core of William Tell creates its own *Sonderbund* (1844) and fires civil war, from which the modern federation of 1848 arises.

A similar fate strikes the age-old Roman Empire of the German Nation. In the German Confederation, successor after Napoleon's intermezzo of the *Reich*, the two rival parts of north and south make war (1866), from which ultimately rises modern Germany. This civil war had an another consequence, interesting for the present theme. In the losing southern confederation a form of flexibility was created between Austria and Hungary, the dual monarchy. This was meant to give Austria a 'hard core' status and allow it to take wage revenge on the Prussians. But this hard core turned out to be just another step in the disintegration of the Habsburg empire, which would end in world war. These examples seem to suggest that the creation of stable cores of groupings between leagues or confederations, in which not a single power has the ambition and/or power to dominate, lead to conceit, irritation and ultimately violence. They are no way to controlled change.

This brings us to consider the 'Franco-German core' in the Union. This has no single leadership. The tandem of Germany and France implies that agreement between these two is a condition for anything to happen in the Union. But this is not the same as saying that this couple is in charge.[7] It is mistaking consequence for cause to think that a number of countries manifesting itself as a core will generate the necessary authority. As long as the Franco-German core fails to show a minor member such as Greece its place for misbehaving in the Balkans or towards Turkey, to which all the means are available, or to press Luxembourg to reason in the subject of tax-evasion, why hope to take on a power such as the UK through technicalities such as flexibility?

---

7 If they play boss the result is trouble, even in minor matters. When France and Germany together wanted to push Belgium's Dehaene upon the others for Commission president, they had to cede to Britain-led opposition.

The 'leadership-model' of flexibility is also in direct contradiction with the spirit and logic of the European Treaties. Far from intending to create for Germany, the leading power by far, either with or without France, a dominant position, these are inspired by the idea to absorb Germany's latent dominance. Each form of physical compulsion or pressure, let alone violence, between the Member States (without which there can be no authority) is ruled out as a matter of principle.

Yet this leadership-model tends to dominate if not the facts then the minds. This is not only because of its clarity and simplicity, but also because the alternative is so opaque. What is the result of flexibility if not greater action capacity of the core? The answer to this question can only be given once it is understood how the negotiations leading up to Amsterdam have in fact proven to be a refusal of the 'leadership model'.

4 Amsterdam

The main feat in the skirmishes leading up to the Amsterdam summit is the gradual watering down and ultimate abandoning of the requirement that exceptions (of core members or of outsiders) be temporary. In the rich imagery coming with the leadership-model, between the lead-group in cycling to convoys and flocks of birds the idea is that all arrive at the same destination. Indeed during the whole IGC-process it was always emphasised that differences should be temporary.[8] But in the Treaty-text the requirement is not to be found.

One may note that the disillusion had already been booked with Monetary Union, which originally established the provisional character of 'derogations' (see Article 122 EC). Yet the Danish and British in Maastricht won the right to keep out even if they complied with the conditions.

The next feat of arms is the requirement that the core be a majority of members, combined with non-exclusion and veto.

- *Majority-core.* In the original proposals the core would consist of a small group of 5-6 countries. It took the protagonists to sit down at Amsterdam before they swallowed the condition that the core must start with at least a majority. The condition is logical, as one could otherwise get rival groups. But it is a defeat for the core-group idea.[9]

- *Non-exclusion.* The principles of non-exclusion and facilitated access (Article 43(g) EU) are hard to reconcile with the idea of a core. In previous suggestions

8 See for the Belgian position, a good example, Duff (ed.), *The Treaty of Amsterdam. Text and Commentary*, London, p. 189.

9 In the EMU transition procedure it is, remarkably, the other way. First a majority is sought. If not found, a minority suffices (Article 121 EC).

(as in EMU) there was a preference for admission-requirements. They have not made it into the text. Then what is to keep an unwilling and/or unable member either to be included in the leading group or to send a few helpers along to frustrate it?

- *Veto.* The picture is completed by the actual veto-power each Member has, to block escapes. This veto-power is on the basis of an adapted formula of the notorious Luxembourg-compromise, to be found in Articles 40, par.2 EU and Article 11, par. 2 EC:

'If a member of the Council declares that, for important and stated reasons of national policy it intends to oppose the granting of an authorisation by qualified majority, a vote shall not be taken. The Council may, acting by a qualified majority, request that the matter be referred to the European Council for decision by unanimity.'

In comparison with the Luxembourg-compromise: 'important *interests'* (my emphasis) this version is favourable to the spoilsport, who does not have to adduce national interests but only national policy, a lighter test. Interestingly he may have to account for his conduct in the European Council at the others' request, but may profitably stick to his guns, as a contrary European Council decision requires unanimity.[10]

A variety of this *over-representation of unwillingness* is to be found in the figure of Article 34, par.2 EU, third pillar conventions. The novelty is entry into force at ratification by half the members. France and Germany hoped to introduce a Schengen-like bypass into the Treaty. The result was perverted by the fact that *conclusion* requires unanimity in the Council, so that spoilsports are required to vote along with the text to be adopted, so they can water it down though they have no intention or obligation to move toward being bound.[11]

To sum up: in the Amsterdam IGC a leadership-form of flexibility has not been adopted but rejected. Exceptions are without a time limit and on the other hand participation is not subject to strict tests. This causes the spoilsports to be present either in the creation of the flexibility, to water it down, or in its application, to be a nuisance. On the one hand the introduction of forms of flexibility is subject to strict conditions for the sake of protecting the Treaties

---

10 Luxembourg compromise: *Bulletin* 3/1966, p. 9.

11 In the Franco-German document of October 17, 1996 addressed at the reflection-group, in which the idea was launched, the term used was 'des conventions à moins de quinze'. To all probability this meant *conclusion* by less than all, as this is the only way to make a reduction in participants lead to a spiriting up of the text. *Europe Documents* 2009/96.

from infection. On the other it is made easy on the unwilling members to frustrate or water down flexible cooperation.[12]

This is not meant, however, to be a negative assessment of Amsterdam. Historical experience suggests, quite to the contrary, that to reject the leadership-model may have been an act of wisdom.

Nice altered the flexibility provisions, but does it accept the leadership-model?

5 Nice

Though Nice was meant to turn the flexibility provisions into a workable device, it still is possible for unwilling members to frustrate the creation of flexible cooperation. The adaptation of the formula of the Luxembourg Agreement has been deleted, but the authorisation decision still may be referred to the European Council. There is no more mention of unanimity in Articles 11 EC and 40a, par. 2 EU. The 'emergency brake' has not completely disappeared; it has at least been made less explicit.

Relaxation of the triggering mechanism can also be found in the altered condition that the core must start with at least eight members. As long as the Union does not take in any new members, it is going against the idea of a core-group. In an enlarged EU creation of a minority core-group will be possible. Since the negotiators were not willing to embrace the leadership-model, they made provisions on non-exclusion and last instance possibility (Articles 43b and 43a EU) more explicit.

After Nice, a core-group can be formed in theory. Nevertheless, the altered treaty provisions are certainly not an acceptation of the leadership-model.

6 Flexibility of balance

So what new technique has been adopted as closer cooperation? One should beware of the 'antinomy-trap'. Rejection of a model does not automatically mean adoption of its terminological opposite. In fact it has been left up to time to show where the Treaty provisions are landing us. But on the other hand the possibilities are not infinite.

12 L.J. Brinkhorst, presently Minister for Agriculture, noticed that flexibility may even have an unintended effect in regard of candidate-members. The idea was to give them the opportunity to keep out of the most advanced areas of common policy. These states in fact will be eager to apply for any form of closer cooperation, irrespective of the consequences, so that it will have to be up to the others to keep them out - for which the rules do not provide the means.

Let us call the adopted model, liberally, the 'flexibility of balance'. This is not a term with great defining force. On the other hand it is not totally without giving an idea of the situation. At least there is no dominant party able to impose its will, nor an established alliance tending to conceit without the will to enforce its vision. There will be no great common acting capacity; the energies available will be spent on negotiations and the game of coalitions. Surely in this model flexibility, or closer cooperation, is essential too.

A balancing model is familiar from two different historical contexts. In the international society it goes under the name of the 'balance of powers', a concept developed by William Temple, F. de Lisola and the stadtholder-king William and practised by the British.[13] In the domestic context it is both more ancient and more recent: one finds it in the doctrine of checks and balances as developed by American constitutionalists (with reference to Montesquieu and Locke), to correct Rousseau-like ideas about democracy. The theorem of checks and balances has deeper roots in feudalism and even reaches down to Aristotle, Polybius and Livy.

In confederations, in between international and domestic political organisation, it is traditional to seek balance. The Swiss example, above, is telling. It has lasted five centuries. The Roman Empire of the German nation is another case. Its stability was found in the flexible relationship between the larger participants on the one hand and the smaller on the other. This empire was flexible to the point of fluidity; it had no fixed centre nor even a fixed territorial definition. A cybernetics expert might call it a 'self-governing system', and historians fight over the question what held it together, but it did last eight hundred years. If constitutional historian Van Caenegem likens the Union to it, it is in part from admiration.[14]

In his brilliant pamphlet *La fin de la démocratie* J.M. Guéhenno asserts that in fact Europe is turning in its state organisation for an imperial one:

'L'Europe ne sera pas une structure institutionnelle figée, assise sur un territoire définitivement borné, mais un élément dans un ensemble d'institutions concurrentes, n'obéissant à aucune architecture claire ... Cette concurrence institutionnelle – conséquence d'une diffusion de la puissance entre plusieurs structures qui se recoupent sans se superposer, qui se complètent sans pouvoir tout à fait éliminer la concurrence – étendra à un ordre politique en voie de disparition les mécanismes de régulation du pouvoir que nous voyons à l'oeuvre dans les entreprises modernes.'[15]

---

[13] F.H. Hinsley, *Power and the Pursuit of Peace*, Cambridge, 1963, p. 160.

[14] R.C. van Caenegem, *An historical introduction to Western Constitutional Law*, Cambridge, 1995, p. 132-133.

[15] Paris 1993, p. 80-81. Guéhenno also refers to a 'sondage récent' which indicates that a majority of Germans sees or wishes its future such as that of a large Switzerland.

This evocative prose of course is more accurate in its pointing out what is in the process of disappearing than what is coming into existence; one must appreciate the author's respect for time. Less restraint we find in a German constitutionalist, Heinz, who asserts that Bismarck's Second German Empire is the brilliant example for the Union's constitutional structure. This Empire was essentially a confederation, with far reaching centralisation of government functions, but without the ambition of *Herrschaft* (authority or sovereignty). It would never have occurred to Bismarck, says Heinz, to have Bavaria outvoted by the others' joined forces. The construct was perverted, writes Heinz, by the democrats' obstinacy in the *Reichstag* (Parliament), which

> *'...gesamtdeutsche Interessen anstelle gemeinsamer Interessen der Mitgliedstaaten förderte und im Verein mit den gesamtdeutschen Bestrebungen Kaiser Wilhelms II. zur einer deutschen Grossmachtpolitik führte, die früher oder später im Weltkriech enden mußte, zunächst aber mit der Förderung preussischen Wesens eine unselige Gleichschaltung der Deutschen Staaten bewirkte.'*[16]

7 Balanced constitution

Some definition may be given to the choice actually made by putting this into the context of other recent constitutional inventions for the Union. These are first the principle of subsidiarity and second the Central Bank's independent status. It is not difficult to see how these two elements do prop up the Union into a proto-political status, while at the same time reducing the perspective of authority. The Union is in fact becoming a close-knit and stable system with a growing number of autonomous centres of decision.[17]

---

[16] K.E. Heinz, "Europäische Zukunft - Bundesstaat oder Staatengemeinschaft?" *DöV* 1994, p. 994-1000; last quotation on p. 1000; also: "Delegation und Mandat. Eine rechts- und Verfassungstheoretische Untersuchung" *Der Staat* 1997, p. 495-520. At the end of the latter, the author gets carried away by the winds of consequence: 'Wer die europäischen Gemeinschaftsstrukturen als unterentwickelt betrachtet, weil sie nicht nach dem Demokratie-Prinzip gestaltet sind, der versteht nicht die epochale Bedeutung des humanen und politischen Fortschritts, der in der Abkehr vond demokratischen entscheidungsstrukturen zugunsten der Verwirklichung von sachlogischer Regelungsprinzipien liegt.' (p. 520). Heinz is awfully enthousiastic about Europe as a pragmatic community of States and his distaste for democratic elements is inspired by an exemplary conception of German history.

[17] See, of this author (ed.) "The Great European Constitutional Shift," in (idem, ed.) *Bastard or Monster. Money, Territory and the Constitution of Europe Amsterdam*, G.K. van Hogendorpcentrum UvA, 1998, p. 107-122.

Daintith, British constitutionalist, has coined for this situation, which he sees to grow out of Monetary Union, the term 'balanced constitution'. The system of balanced power provides a check on the 'democratic principle' of majority power as found in democratic systems such as the US and the Federal Republic.[18]

In the context of Europe, which has no democratic majority-system, the 'balanced constitution' is not functioning as a check but in its own right. The objective is not so much to prevent the growth of power but to prevent violence by absorbing shocks, respecting essential interests and furthering a certain evolution. It is less a goal-oriented system than one meant to consolidate relationships by introducing limited impulses to change, more or less in the way a set of people condemned to live in proximity will set itself tasks just to avoid the members' flying at each other and to ensure a change of guard and of responsibilities. Flexibility and equipoise are no recipe for authority but for reflection, delay, stability. Hence the motto 'roseau réflichissant' (reflecting reed) for this piece.

Two questions remain. What does such a balanced model look like and how does it work; what does it offer a country as The Netherlands.

As to the first question, this is up to time to answer. It is right to realise that Europe is becoming a constitutional *terra incognita*. This is nothing to worry about, as the continent has always been a constitutional laboratory and it will meet this test also. Second, it is good to know that human ingenuity is limited and that it will always need to seek recourse to proven solutions. Third, a regression to 'imperial' situations, however strong the inclination, is probably unacceptable to modern and 'enlightened' Western man.[19] But in order to see through the fast growing bush of legal complexity, ingenuity is needed more and more.

Then the Dutch position. Flexibility is a token but furnishes no cogent structure. The classical federalist future of Europe is (if it ever was) now past. This removes the ground under the old Dutch Europe-coalition between federalists, legal science and business, not to forget the law firms.

Politically it suggests for us to withdraw from the Franco-German 'armpit' (the image of warmth and shelter which was in vogue for a while). But lawyers too should read the signs and be prepared to look at the situation in a new spirit. If only in order to find a new coalition of facts and ideas working for the Dutch interests.

I think the Home and Foreign ministries should undertake or support together a project of historical and comparative constitutional study, for the purpose of better understanding the situation having arisen, and to get the most out of its quite limited amenability to be ordered.

---

[18] T. Daintith, "Between Domestic Democracy and an Alien Rule of Law? Some Thoughts on the Independence of the Bank of England", *Public Law*, 1995, p. 118-132, at p. 131.

[19] It was Bruno de Witte who pointed this out to me.

List of Abbreviations

BL	Grundgesetz (Basic Law, Germany)
CDU	Christlich Demokratische Union
CIS	Commonwealth of Independent States
CMLRev	Common Market Law Review
CFSP	Common Foreign and Security Policy
CSU	Christlich-Soziale Union
DöV	Die öffentliche Verwaltung
EC	European Community
ECR	European Court Reports
EMU	Economic and Monetary Union
EU	European Union
GDR	German Democratic Republic
IGC	Intergovernmental Conference
jo.	juncto
NATO	North Atlantic Treaty Organisation
RMUE	Revue du Marché Unique Européen
SEW	Sociaal Economische Wetgeving
TOM	territoires d'outre mer
UK	United Kingdom
UN	Untited Nations
US(A)	United States (of America)
WEU	Western European Union
WRR	Wetenschappelijke Raad voor het Regeringsbeleid
ZDF	Zweites Deutsches Fernsehen

Index

Contributors

Contributors

Margreth de Bonth

Margreth de Bonth graduated in European Studies at the University of Amsterdam. She wrote a thesis on the concept of sovereignty. She is currently working as a researcher at the Schoordijk Institute of Tilburg University, The Netherlands. She prepares a doctoral thesis on the right to development as a human right.

Timothy J. Conlan

Timothy J. Conlan is an Associate Professor of Government and Politics at George Mason University. He holds a Ph.D. in Government from Harvard University and an A.B. degree in Political science from the University of Chicago. During 1998, he was a Fullbright Scholar at Erasmus University Rotterdam. His works include *From Federalism to Devolution: Twenty Five Years of International Reform* (Washington: Brookings Institution, 1998), and *International Dimensions of American Federalism: State Policy Responses to a Changing Global Environment* (Lexington, KY: Council of State Governments, 1997).

Tom Eijsbouts

Tom Eijsbouts is director of the G.K. van Hogendorp Centre. He is professor in European Constitutional Law and its History at the University of Amsterdam.

Flora Goudappel

Flora Goudappel holds a Ph. D. from Erasmus University Rotterdam, on the subject *Powers and Control Mechanisms in European Federal Systems.* She worked as a senior researcher at the Netherlands School of Social and Economic Policy Research of the University of Utrecht. Her research areas are federalism, European constitutional and competition law, as well as Dutch and European education law. At present, she is legal advisor at the Ministry of Justice of The Netherlands.

Annemarie Lansdaal

Annemarie Lansdaal was assistant to the G.K. van Hogendorp Centre at the time of the conference. She wrote her undergraduate thesis on flexibility: *Flexibilité, la signification et l'évolution du terme au cours de la Conférence intergouvernementale de 1996.* (Amsterdam University, august 1998). At present, she works for Niehe and Lancée consultancy.

Roel Pieterman

Roel Pieterman teaches sociology of law at Erasmus University Rotterdam. His dissertation (1990) is a treatise on the political and legal debates in the nineteenth century on the position of the judiciary in the division of powers in the state. Since then he has also published on the relevance of social theory for legal thought and on socio-legal theory. Research subjects on which he published include the regulation of euthanasia and organ donation.

Annette Schrauwen

Annette Schrauwen is a lecturer in European Politics and European Law at the Faculty of Law of the University of Amsterdam She wrote a dissertation (1997) on the concept of the Internal market. Her research area is free movement within the European Union, publications include "Sink or Swim together? Developments in European Citizenship", *Fordham International Law Journal*, Vol. 23, March 2000, p. 778-794

Elies Steyger

Elies Steyger has been legal counsel to respectively the Minister of Public Health and Social Services, and the Minister of Economic Affairs since 1991. Before that she worked as an associate Professor at the University of Maastricht. At present, she works as a lawyer at the law firm of Pels Rijcken & Drooglever Fortuijn in the Hague and she is Professor in European administrative law at the Vrije Universiteit in Amsterdam. She has published several books and Articles on constitutional and administrative law of the European Union, and on the chances for survival of national traditions in the case law of the Court of Justice.

Bruno De Witte

Bruno De Witte holds a Ph. D. in Law from the European University Institute in Florence (*The Protection of Linguistic Diversity through Fundamental Rights* - 1985). From 1985-1989 he was assistant Professor at the European University Institute in Florence. Currently, he is Professor of European Law and holds a Jean Monnet Chair at the Rijksuniversiteit Limburg. He published widely on the nature of European Community Law and its relationship with constitutional law and public international law; European Community Law and policy in the field of education, culture, media and language.

G.J.M. van Wissen

G.J.M. van Wissen is professor of comparative constitutional law at the Faculty of Law of the University of Amsterdam. He is specialised in German constitutional law and in the constitutional law of the countries of Central and Eastern Europe. Professor dr. van Wissen is director of the Amsterdam Institute of Law Education at the Faculty of Law.